THE MYTH
OF FREE TRADE

THE MYTH
OF FREE TRADE

PATTERNS OF PROTECTIONISM SINCE 1945

Harry Shutt

BASIL BLACKWELL

THE ECONOMIST BOOKS

First published 1985

Basil Blackwell Ltd
108 Cowley Road, Oxford OX4 1JF, UK.
and
The Economist Publications Ltd.
40 Duke Street, London W1M 5DG.

British Library Cataloguing in Publication Data

Shutt, Harry
  The myth of free trade : patterns of
protectionism since 1945.
  1. Free trade and protection
  I. Title
  382.7   HF1713

ISBN 0-631-13997-4

Library of Congress Cataloging in Publication Data

Shutt, Harry.
  The myth of free trade.

  Includes index
  1. Free trade and protection.   I. Title.
HF1713.S52   1985   382.7   84-28408
ISBN 0-631-13997-4

Typeset by Saxon, Derby.
Printed in Great Britain by Page Bros., Norwich

Contents

CHAPTER 1

The Limits of Delusion

Doublethink means the power of holding contradictory beliefs in one's mind simultaneously, and accepting both of them. . . . To tell deliberate lies while genuinely believing in them, to forget any fact that has become inconvenient, and then, when it becomes necessary again, to draw it back from oblivion for just as long as it is needed, to deny the existence of objective reality and all the while to take account of the reality which one denies – all this is indispensably necessary.

George Orwell, *1984*.

The steady growth of state intervention has been sponsored and administered by political leaders who were all the time proclaiming the virtues of a free economy.

Gunnar Mydral, *Beyond the Welfare State*.

It would be hard to find anyone today who would seriously advance the claim that the developed industrialized economies of the Western World are run according to principles closely resembling those of the free market. Indeed a passing acquaintance with economic theory, as portrayed in any modern standard textbook, convinces us that conditions of perfect competition can never be attained in the real world, with the clear implication that the theoretical benefits of the free market can in practice only be secured, at best, in an extremely qualified form.

Furthermore, few would dispute that for most of the period since World War II it has been the prevailing opinion that it was not even desirable that it should be left to the market – however 'perfect' or imperfect its operation might have been – to determine the pattern and scale of economic activity. Instead it has been the consensus, at least until fairly recently, that if governments are to maintain full employment – seen in the post-war era as the supreme objective of national economic policy – they must intervene in the economy in such a way as to 'offset the irreducible fluctuations in the private sector of the market'.[1]

Yet if there has been general agreement as to the need for state intervention there has been much less as to the form it should or should not take or the degree to which it might properly be applied. Consequently much state intervention has been of an informal and *ad hoc* nature – a fact which has arguably made it easier to sustain the belief that market forces are still the dominant influence in determining the allocation of resources and the distribution of rewards. The result was that the so-called mixed economy structure was riddled with inconsistencies and inequities – a fact well documented by Professor Galbraith in the 1950s and 1960s. For a long time, however, these anomalies were not a source of serious concern or friction either within or between nations. It may be inferred that such acceptance was made possible by the general climate of prosperity and expansion which prevailed throughout the industrialized 'market' economies for virtually the whole of the period from the end of the war until the early 1970s. As in the Caucus-race in *Alice in Wonderland*, nobody particularly minded that all the participants were playing the game according to different rules as long as there were prizes for everyone.

The notion that the free market was still the basis of Western economic organization was further reinforced by the structure of international economic relations which was established at the end of the war and which remains theoretically in force to date. This has been based upon the principle of the free flow both of trade in goods and services and of capital across frontiers, as well as – until 1971 – on more or less fixed rates of currency exchange. These principles were enshrined at the global level in the General Agreement on Tariffs and Trade (GATT) and in the rules of the International Monetary Fund (IMF) and subsequently reinforced (in relation to exchanges between the industrialized nations) by the Convention of the Organization for Economic Cooperation and Development (OECD).

The progressive lowering or removal of traditional barriers to trade – tariffs and quotas – which was fostered by these institutions during the 1950s and 1960s (a period of sustained expansion without precedent in the industrialized West) lent much credence to the classical view that free trade was the key to economic prosperity. Yet what was hardly perceived, or if perceived seldom emphasized, was that this ostensibly liberal structure of international economic organization was open to manipulation and distortion precisely by means of those interventionist practices which had been effectively legitimized in the context of domestic economic policy – and which indeed were generally perceived as an equally essential condition of prosperity. Again, however, such distortions provoked few objections while the general economic boom continued, and in any case were not apparent – at least until the late 1970s – on such a scale as to weaken the general belief that international free trade was not only an unalloyed benefit but an undoubted reality.

The underlying contradiction in this combination of interventionism in domestic economic management and liberalism in international exchanges was perhaps most conspicuous in the conduct of relations between rich and poor countries (though even there it was still rarely articulated). The reason for this was the obvious relative disadvantage of the less developed countries (LDCs) in competing on equal terms with industrialized nations having an endowment superior to their own in such factors as capital availability, technology, management skills and the size of their domestic market base. While these handicaps were to some extent allowed for in the rules of the GATT and other international institutions, the weight of official opinion in the developed countries, and in the international agencies charged with promoting 'development', was that the adoption of liberal economic policies offered the best hope of raising the LDCs' living standards to the levels enjoyed in the industrialized world and that, conversely, attempts to restrict the impact of market forces would retard this process.

The fact that this advice usually emanated from countries which were themselves protecting their agricultural industries with massive subsidies – frequently to the detriment of LDCs' exports and even in some cases, through the dumping of surpluses, disrupting their domestic markets – was an anomaly which was insufficient to weaken the commitment to the idea of free trade among development economists. For the most part, indeed, they resolutely refused to consider protectionism in terms other than those of the instruments of direct trade control (tariffs, import deposits, exchange controls, quotas and licensing). It was even possible, at least until the early 1970s, to write whole books purporting to measure the extent of 'effective protection' without considering the impact of other market-distorting practices – except by implication to dismiss their significance. 'In an indirect way, the extent of protection is also affected by other types of policy measures, such as profits taxes, credit policy and social security arrangements. These, however, fall outside the scope of the present inquiry, which is concerned with *protective measures proper*'.[2] It is perhaps only fair to point out that such omissions are largely conditioned by the extreme difficulty, if not impossibility, of quantifying the protectionist impact of indirect measures such as credit restrictions. This point has been acknowledged by others who have sought to compare the levels of protectionism in different countries,[3] although this has not necessarily prevented their results from being taken as a realistic basis for international comparisons. This may be seen as an illustration of an all too familiar weakness of contemporary economics – the tendency to assume that only those variables which can be quantified are of real importance.

Such bland perversity became more difficult to sustain, however, as the post-war boom dissolved into recession after 1973. Ever since then there has been an increasingly pronounced tendency on the part of all countries to resort to market-distorting expedients in an attempt to avert the worst effects of the downturn. At the same time, the rapid advance of new technology – transforming the pattern of production and costs in many industries – has made the governments of industrialized countries fearful of losing out in the race to benefit from the 'second industrial revolution' and has consequently been an added spur to interventionism.

The result has been a proliferation among all industrialized countries – and to a lesser extent among LDCs as well – of fiscal incentives and direct subsidies to investment (either general or selective), government-funded research and development programmes, official underwriting of loans to and losses incurred by the private sector, and various other supports to production and investment. On top of this there has been increasingly uninhibited resort to the direct subvention of exports by such means as

subsidized credit insurance and the selective use of grants disguised as development aid.

At the same time, faced with the painful reality of chronic and
increasing oversupply in such traditional manufacturing sectors as
steel, shipbuilding and motor vehicles, and unable to contemplate
either the scale of redundancies implied in a market-based
rationalisation or the mounting fiscal burden of continuing direct
subsidies, governments have been forced to seek more direct
restraints on imports. These have tended to take the form of
agreements by the more competitive exporters – who are frequently found to be Japanese – to limit their shipments to a particular
market. Such a tacit evasion of the GATT rules – which in some
cases amounts to the virtual cartelization of the market, often
backed up by *de facto* minimum price thresholds – is usually made
easier by the acquiescence of the supplier, who is consoled for his
loss of market share by the fact that his decreased volume of sales
will obtain higher unit prices. Likewise the process is reinforced by
the policies of the multinational companies, whose response to the
increased competitive pressures of the recession is to seek closer
collaboration among themselves and thus limit competition even
further.

These developments have made it progressively more difficult to
maintain the fiction that world trade is governed by a system of
rules which assures the open and non-discriminatory exchange of
goods and services, as it is supposed to be according to the
principles of the GATT. Indeed it has become clear that governments see less and less merit in adhering to the concept of open
trade where they perceive that it is manifestly damaging to their
own or their country's interests to do so, particularly when it is
apparent that other countries are showing progressively less
respect for the idea of free trade. The temptation to follow their
example is all the greater once it is recognized that to do so does
not necessarily entail flouting the rules of the GATT. In this way
the crumbling of the commitment to the spirit, if not the letter, of
the GATT system can be seen to feed on itself, once there have
been enough well-publicized demonstrations of loss of faith in it.

This manifest fragility of what was supposed to be a firm and
widespread belief in the benefits of free trade, and the ready
espousal of protectionism by so many countries, have provoked
growing expressions of concern – indeed of alarm – from a large

number of world leaders, representing international agencies and multinational companies as well as national governments. Typical of these has been the warning of the Brandt Commission (established in the late 1970s to examine the plight of the world's poor countries) that 'protectionism threatens the future of the world economy and is inimical to the interests of developing and developed countries alike'.[4] In similar vein the World Bank's World Development Report of 1982 declared that 'nothing is more likely to jeopardize the strong growth momentum built up over the last 30 years than a renewal of protectionism', while the OECD Council of Ministers at their 1983 meeting concluded that 'strengthening the open and multilateral trading system is essential to support the recovery and the transition to sustained growth'. A still more emphatic endorsement of this consensus was given at the Williamsburg summit of Western leaders in 1983 with the unequivocal pronouncement, 'We commit ourselves to halt protectionism'.

Despite these stern and seemingly unanimous exhortations from every quarter of the international establishment there is no sign of any slowing down, let alone reversal, of the trend towards manipulated and 'managed' trade. If anything, indeed, the process is accelerating. Thus the contrast between official theory and official practice – between 'rhetoric and reality' – is becoming more blatant than ever.

It is the purpose of this book to chart and explain this divergence. Its underlying thesis is that, so far from freedom of trade being a condition of prosperity, the reverse is actually the case. As a consequence nations will engage in free and open trade only to the extent that they perceive it will pay them to do so. In short, most governments follow Disraeli's dictum that liberalism should be regarded as an expedient not a principle. This explains why 'while economic theory demonstrates the welfare-superiority of free trade, only Britain, in the late nineteenth century, has tried it'.[5]

Yet while it will be made clear that free trade has only ever existed in a very qualified sense and that efforts to 'restore' it in a period of world recession are at best wholly futile – and in many cases lacking in sincerity – this should not be taken to suggest that the anarchy which is now spreading through the international economy can be regarded with equanimity or passive resignation, let alone approval. Indeed it is one of the author's principal contentions that the uncoordinated acts of intervention undertaken by individual governments – in defiance of the dictates of market forces – have produced conditions of dangerous instability. Yet this position cannot be rectified, nor can a degree of rationality be restored to economic planning and corporate mangement, as long as the participants feel it necessary to pretend that they are or should be operating under a system of free trade.

The alternative to abandoning this notion in favour of reality is a further extension of covert protectionism and the consequent perpetuation of imbalance and oversupply in world markets. Those who continue instead to believe that this problem can and will be resolved by a return to sustained high rates of economic growth – an occurrence which is increasingly looked for in hope rather than on the basis of reasoned prediction – have still to explain how such growth can possibly be fast enough to absorb the ever more rapid rise in the world's productive capacity, fuelled by the relentless advance of technology.

In the probable absence of such an economic miracle the disjunction between demand and supply in world markets seems set to increase to the point where it precipitates a major world financial collapse, with potentially catastrophic consequences for rich and poor nations alike. This book seeks to show that such a disaster can only be averted and stability restored if it is openly accepted that world trade must be to a large extent planned instead of being left at the mercy of increasingly unfree and unfair market forces. Such planning would clearly have to go beyond the present isolated and covert attempts at control and management of markets currently being perpetrated by both multinational companies and governments. Rather it must be coordinated within the framework of some form of agreed allocation of resources and division of labour among nations. Those who resist this conclusion must reconcile themselves to an ever greater reliance on the weapons of distortion and subterfuge. They may in this event think it appropriate, in the post-1984 world, to coin a new Orwellian slogan: PROTECTIONISM IS FREE TRADE.

NOTES
(1) International Labour Office, *Action Against Unemployment.*
   Geneva 1950.

(2) B. Balassa and Associates, *The Structure of Protection in Developing Countries.* Baltimore. John Hopkins Press 1971 (author's emphasis).
(3) S.A.B. Page, *The Management of International Trade.* London. National Institute of Economic and Social Research 1979.
(4) Brandt Commission, *North–South: A Programme for Survival.* London. Pan Books 1980.
(5) W.M. Scammel, *The International Economy since 1945.* London. Macmillan 1980.

CHAPTER 2

The Post-War Commitment to Free Trade

The notion that the practice of free trade is an essential feature of any economic order capable of maximizing the well-being of the world's population has probably never enjoyed such widespread and sustained acceptance – at least to judge from the official pronouncements of national governments and international agencies – as it has since World War II. The breadth and durability of this consensus may be ascribed to a number of factors, which we shall examine in more detail later in this chapter. However, in order to appreciate its full significance it is appropriate to try and set it in the context of the history of international trade and economic relations since the Industrial Revolution.

The most striking point of contrast between the conduct of international trade before World War II and that since was the absence in the earlier period of any effective structure of international economic organization which was both truly global in scope – rather than confined to discrete groups of states linked in political associations of one kind or another – and at the same time endowed with some kind of formal system of rules and a quasi-legal authority to enforce them. It is true that between the wars the League of Nations had theoretically been intended to provide a basis for promoting greater international economic cooperation, but it never established any kind of institutional framework which might have been expected to make a reality of this intention. Indeed its only efforts in this direction consisted of a number of *ad hoc* international conferences[1] at which lip-service was ritually paid to the desirability of non-discriminatory free trade, yet which totally failed in practice to achieve any breaking down of the barriers between trading blocs – barriers which on the contrary became greater than ever during the Great Depression of the 1930s.

MERCANTILISM BEFORE WORLD WAR I

Indeed by common consent the restrictions on international trade and payments were much greater throughout the inter-war period than they were before 1914. This was the consequence of the disruption and devastation caused by the Great War, whose impact was perpetuated well beyond its immediate aftermath by the burden of reparations imposed on Germany and the other defeated nations of Central Europe. In consequence these countries were forced on to the economic defensive following the signing of the Treaty of Versailles and had no choice but to limit severely their freedom of exchange with other countries during the 1920s – and more than ever after the world collapse of 1929-31.

Yet although the 50 years prior to World War I were by contrast a broadly expansionary phase in international trade – to some extent, perhaps, under the impetus of British adoption of a free trade posture from 1860 – there was arguably still less of a consensus among most major trading nations in favour either of non-discrimination or of lower tariff barriers than prevailed between the two world wars. Indeed of the two countries which emerged during the late nineteenth Century as the principal challengers to Great Britain's economic dominance – the United States and Germany – the former steadily raised its tariffs between 1860 and 1900, while the latter largely forged its unity, before the proclamation of the German Empire in 1871, on the basis of a discriminatory customs union among the traditional German states (the Zollverein) and subsequently adopted a high tariff policy towards the rest of the world.

In fact, although the nineteenth century is generally thought to have been the classic age of economic liberalism – in contrast to the restrictive mercantilist attitudes which had previously governed the economies of Europe – closer examination shows that, whatever the views of contemporary economists and men of business may have been, those in control of governments saw good reasons for maintaining a tight grip on foreign trade. For even if mercantilism in the limited classical sense of the term – that is, giving primacy to increasing the national stock of bullion – had generally been rejected, governments, particularly those of the then newly emergent nation states, still retained a large measure of what Adam Smith[2] would have seen as the mercantilist spirit. That is to say that they saw a clear link between economic and commercial strength on the one hand and national political power on the other, and they consequently regarded the pattern of trade flows as something too important to be left at the mercy of the uncertain industriousness and acumen of their labour force or what Lord Keynes later termed the 'animal spirits' of their entrepreneurs.

Clearly Great Britain – at that time by far the world's premier trading nation – was a striking exception to this general rule in the half-century up to 1914. Yet it can scarcely be denied that it was only because it felt itself to be so economically dominant that it could afford to throw its market completely open – a move which in any case was only made in the teeth of powerful domestic opposition. It is also surely significant that this period proved to be the beginning of the end of British commercial pre-eminence and also the prelude to the eclipse of the Whig/Liberal party which had been the supreme advocate and architect of the free trade policy.

It may thus reasonably be claimed that, viewed from a global standpoint, the pattern of international trade continued to be heavily influenced by broadly mercantilist rather than liberal influences from the Industrial Revolution right up to World War II. Equally, however, there is no denying that the major Western nations emerged from that conflict more visibly determined than at any previous time to repudiate protectionism and embrace free trade. As will be demonstrated throughout this book, there are serious grounds for doubting how far the immediate post-war vision ever became a reality; yet there can be little doubt of the commitment of the architects of the post-war international economic system to make it so.

WORLD WAR II AND THE EMERGENCE OF THE GATT

What was it that made World War II such a watershed in international attitudes? Undoubtedly a major factor, if not the decisive one, was the widespread belief that the nationalist/ mercantilist approach to international economic relations had been a significant contributing cause of the war. In other words, just as the First World War had appeared to show the need for international collective military security (which it had, of course, been the purpose of the League of Nations to provide), so an important lesson of the Second was perceived to be the need for economic collective security – or at least to avoid any repetition of the pre-war tendency to pursue national economic policy goals through the instrument of commercial discrimination against other countries.

Yet while the importance of such idealism in the aftermath of the most destructive war in history should not be underrated, other equally crucial but more narrowly practical considerations were also involved. In particular the United States, which emerged from the war in a position of such overwhelming superiority – both military and economic – *vis-à-vis* the rest of the Western World that it could largely dictate the pattern of the new post-war order, found itself for the first time in its history having something tangible to gain from free trade. This was because, like Britain in 1860, she had developed an industrial and technological capability which no other country could begin to match – particularly as all her potential competitors had suffered either massive physical destruction of their industrial infrastructure during the war or (as in the case of Britain) a massive financial drain which inhibited efforts at re-equipping for peacetime economic activity, whereas the US economy, by contrast, had been given a tremendous stimulus by the war.

This consequent US enthusiasm for free trade in 1945, strongly contrasting as it did with that country's previously strongly protectionist tendencies, was naturally not so wholeheartedly endorsed by other Western nations, including Britain – the other principal architect of the post-war economic order, though in practice very much a junior partner to the vastly stronger United States. Indeed, since the relative buoyancy of its economy in the

1930s obviously owed much to the possession of a captive market for industrial products in the Commonwealth and Empire based on the preference system inaugurated by the Ottawa Agreements of 1932, Britain was bound to oppose the full-blooded application of non-discrimination. Moreover it is noteworthy that the great Lord Keynes, the most prestigious economist of the time and Britain's chief negotiator at the Bretton Woods conference which laid the foundations of the post-war economic system, expressed more fundamental reservations as to the desirability of basing the world order on the free trade principle. Writing to a fellow British official in 1944, he stated his belief that 'the future lies with:

(i) State trading for commodities;
(ii) International cartels for necessary manufactures; and
(iii) Quantitative import restrictions for non-necessary manufactures.'[3]

In view of such scepticism and of more widespread resistance from the economically weaker nations it may seem remarkable that it was possible to get general acceptance of the need for a global system of free trade based on non-discrimination. It may well be, in fact, that it would have got no further than the polite lip-service of the 1920s but for the presence of another, wholly new, ingredient in the post-war scheme of things. This was the agreement, hammered out at Bretton Woods and at subsequent negotiations held between 1944 and 1946, for a global system of foreign exchange and payments based on the newly created International Monetary Fund (IMF). For by introducing an unprecedented mechanism for cooperative management of balance of payments deficits it greatly reduced the possibiility that these might seriously inhibit the economic freedom and expansion of those countries affected by them – provided at least that they were cyclical or short term in nature. With the threat of damaging runs on their respective currencies thus much diminished, many countries were undoubtedly far more amenable to exposing their economies to foreign competition than they would otherwise have been.[4]

Yet even in spite of this climate more favourable to open trading relationships than ever before it was, not surprisingly, difficult to secure agreement on a generally applicable set of rules capable of being formally enshrined in a treaty which could be signed by the majority of countries. This explains why the General Agreement on Tariffs and Trade (GATT) was not finalized until 1948 – some two years after the shape of the rest of the 'Bretton Woods system' had been agreed – and then in a form much less ambitious than had been envisaged by its champions in the Truman administration. In fact the final shape of the GATT may be seen as the outcome of a prolonged retreat from the initial code agreed in principle at an Anglo-American seminar held in 1943, when the outlines of what was intended to be a more enlightened post-war world first began to be sketched out by the Western allies.[5]

There is a tendency on the part of certain American economists[6] to present the resulting compromise, as well as many of the subsequent derogations from the principles of GATT, as stemming from a US desire to make concessions to its less liberal trading partners in the interests of greater Western political solidarity. Yet while many countries of different degrees of economic strength and competitive potential did raise objections to a more open structure on a number of grounds, the most telling comment on contemporary perceptions as to the ultimate viability of genuine global free trade is provided by the harsh truth that the United States itself – far and away the strongest country of all – finally baulked at applying the principles its own administration had itself been loudest in advocating. The most conspicuous crack in this facade of US liberalism occurred after the signing in March 1948 of the Havana Charter, which was intended to lead to the establishment of an International Trade Organization (ITO) – comparable, in its authority to regulate trade, with the IMF in relation to monetary questions. For any prospect this hard-won agreement had of being consummated – requiring as it did ratification by at least 20 countries – was destroyed when it was thrown out by the US Congress, a blow to the prestige of the American administration scarcely less devastating than the congressional rejection of League of Nations membership after World War I.

If the political will to implement anything approaching thoroughgoing free trade was lacking in the United States – a country with a strong tradition of belief in *laissez-faire* principles as well as enormous commercial and political muscle – it is scarcely to be wondered at that other countries with less obvious reason to support it should have shown serious reservations. It was indeed to try and accommodate these that the discussions on the shape of the proposed International Trade Organisation had dragged on until 1948. In doing so they threw up a number of problems which, it may seem with the benefit of hindsight, might have suggested the fundamental impracticability of trying to formulate a set of rules for free trade which was universally acceptable to all countries – that is, at different levels of development and with different social and political priorities.

An illustration of this point is provided by the approach to the proposed 'employment clause' which many nations wished to see incorporated in the rules of the ITO. The idea was to enshrine in it the principle that the maintenance of full employment was a policy objective of such overriding importance that any commitment to free trade might be subordinated to it should the need arise. This was a view strongly upheld by the British Labour government (vigorously supported by Australia and New Zealand), which had both a powerful political commitment to full employment and a fear – which proved to be only too justified – that its weak external position, resulting mainly from the distorting effects of the war, would be rendered still more vulnerable by exposure to free trade. This fear was all the stronger in view of the need to make sterling fully covertible, on which the US began to insist as soon as the war was over – and which was anyway implicit in its reserve currency role in relation to the IMF. In contrast to this view of the primacy of the full employment objective, the United States, where Congress had specifically rejected any formal commitment to pursue this goal at home, [7] was not surprisingly reluctant to endorse it in the context of international relations.

This dispute was finally resolved by a compromise which – though arguably inevitable, particularly in view of the difficulty in reaching an objective definition of full employment – effectively blurred the issue. This was the acceptance of an escape clause, eventually incorporated in the GATT (Article XII), which permitted member countries to apply temporary import controls in the event of serious balance of payments difficulties. Since this also failed, again perhaps unavoidably, to define the meaning of this condition with any precision,[8] it effectively left countries with the option of pursuing full employment at the cost of a deteriorating balance of payments, which they could then use as the excuse for suspending free access to their markets.

Thus perhaps unwittingly the founding fathers of the GATT exposed a fundamental anomaly in the whole argument for free trade – an anomaly which, as will be demonstrated throughout this book, has become more and more glaring in subsequent decades. For it was obvious that no universally applicable set of rules was likely to be freely and indefinitely accepted by countries which did not regard them as both consistent with their ability to pursue their domestic social and economic goals, and at the same time capable of being applied in a way which was seen to be more or less fair. Yet there appears to have been no open recognition of, let alone any attempt to come to grips with, the conundrum which lay at the heart of the 'employment clause' issue, namely that the way in which a country chose to manage its domestic economy was inextricably linked – for example, through its rate of inflation or rate of exchange – with the terms on which its industries could compete in an open international marketplace. Thus countries which, for whatever reason, placed a relatively low premium on assuring full employment or on maintaining reasonable minimum living standards through a form of welfare state, could – other things being equal – attain a lower industrial cost structure than than their more socially compassionate competitors.

It is obvious that it was fears of such restriction on national freedom of action, in relation to a whole range of policy areas, which prevented the International Trade Organization from becoming a reality. They also ensured, by the same token, that the GATT would be an inherently fragile arrangement and that its success would depend – in the absence of any coercive powers – on the continuing recognition by a sufficient number of major trading nations that it was in their interests to continue broadly complying with the spirit if not the letter of the Agreement despite manifest anomalies and inequities in its operation. Given this somewhat unpromising outlook at its inception it might well be argued that the achievements of the GATT in substantially holding the line against protectionism for over a generation up to the mid-1970s have been remarkable indeed. For not only has the

GATT provided a code of practice for international trade and a forum for resolving trade disputes – without which it may confidently be asserted that international commercial relations would have lapsed into chaos much earlier than they did – it has even succeeded in bringing about a progressive reduction in tariffs such that when the latest series of cuts (the Tokyo Round) is fully implemented in 1987 the average tariff levels of all the major industrial nations will have been reduced to a mere 2-3 per cent, compared with 50-60 per cent in some cases in the 1940s.

Yet equally it has to be said that much of the GATT's apparent success in achieving tariff reductions was made possible by the ability of countries to attain protectionist objectives by other means, many of which might hardly have been thought of at the time the Agreement was first formulated. It is true that the GATT is fairly explicit and theoretically strict on the question of dumping (Article VI), and provides for the imposition of countervailing duties against foreign imports which it can be proved have been dumped (that is sold at below the domestic price charged for them in the country of origin), although it is often so difficult and costly to prove a case of dumping that many victims of it prefer to respond by taking equally illegal counter-measures. But it is a measure of the inherent weakness of the Agreement that its attitude to straight subsidies (Article XVI) is not nearly as severe: it seeks to control them by enjoining the governments which are providing them to report such deviations to the GATT secretariat so that their duration can be monitored and steps be taken to ensure their eventual phasing out. Indeed the 1955 version of the Agreement categorically states that such subsidies are all to cease by the beginning of 1958. This apparent ingenuousness would seem to suggest that it had never occurred to the administration of GATT that it was the possibility of applying such subsidies, in the broadest sense of the term, which provided the safety valve vital to the long-term endurance of the whole Agreement.[9] By the 1970s it was no longer possible to ignore the all-pervasive nature of subsidies and other thinly disguised forms of protectionism, which came to be lumped together in official parlance under the heading of non-tariff barriers (NTBs). They were the subject of exhaustive discussion during the Tokyo Round negotiations between 1974 and 1979, as a result of which codes of practice were drawn up which sought to eliminate protectionist action under the following headings:-

(1) Customs valuation (that is, the undue inflating of landed values of imports by customs so as to increase the impact of *ad valorem* import tariffs);
(2) Government procurement (the granting of preference to local suppliers in respect of government contracts without due regard to considerations of competitiveness);
(3) Import licensing procedures (a form of protectionism by delay);
(4) Subsidies and countervailing duties (see later);
(5) Technical barriers to trade (the application of official product specifications and standards so as to limit the ability of foreign suppliers to compete).

The exhaustive codification of those types of market-distorting subsidy which might affect international trade was, not surprisingly, a task which the GATT secretariat felt was beyond them, and the best they could do was to provide an 'illustrative' list of such subsidies while defining the procedure to be followed before applying any countervailing duties against them. A better measure of the scale of the problem, however, is a reference in a later GATT report to its work in updating the inventory of non-tariff measures affecting trade, which was prepared as background data to the Tokyo Round negotiations. It points out that this list included 'hundreds' of non-tariff measures, notified by governments as obstacles to their exports or as unfair advantages to their competitors.[10] Moreover, it may be presumed that this swelling list was itself just the tip of the iceberg, since many governments were probably reticent in complaining about abuses which they also practised themselves. The fact that the secretariat saw fit to keep secret the details of these complaints – on the ostensible grounds that they were confidential information for negotiators – is also perhaps not without significance, since to reveal them might well have been thought likely to highlight the growing disarray in the once calm and supposedly orderly system of open world trade and, worse still, to create a 'bandwagon effect' among those countries which might have felt there was no longer anything to be gained by sticking to the rules.

But if the inherent inability of the GATT to cope with the multifarious forms of non-tariff barriers which governments were able to devise was not exposed until the 1970s – for reasons which will be explained more fully in a later chapter – it became apparent very early in its life that it was going to be applied in a way which could not be reasonably construed as universally fair or non-discriminatory. This was because from 1950 – largely at the instance of the United States, though without any noticeable dissent from Britain or other major industrial nations – it was decided that the rules of GATT should not apply to agriculture. The immediate cause of this modification was the existence of large farm surpluses in the US while at the same time prices to American farmers were being maintained at levels which were above those prevailing on the open world market. There was of course nothing new or uniquely American in the contention that agriculture is a sector of the economy which is peculiarly unsuited to being exposed to the free play of international market forces. The case is generally held to rest on the twin argument that agricultural production is liable to large and uncontrollable fluctuations in output because of its susceptibility to climatic variations and disease, and at the same time is an essential or 'strategic' industry in the sense that food supply is a vital necessity to any economy, so that no country can afford to be dependent on imports for all, or even most, of its food requirements.

Unfortunately, however sound these arguments may appear from a purely national point of view, applied in the context of the GATT they had the effect of weakening its claim to be an equitable system of rules which did not discriminate in favour of or against any particular country or group. For it should have been obvious that by authorizing subsidization and protection of agriculture in industrialized countries where the farm sector was relatively uncompetitive, the GATT Council was imposing an unfair burden on those member states whose comparative advantage lay precisely in that sector – and which indeed, by the same token, were very often those least competitive in manufacturing or services.

It is true that in the early days of the GATT this inequity adversely affected a relatively small number of the 25 or so member countries, and that many of these (for example, Australia, New Zealand and South Africa) were still cushioned from its effects by their privileged access to the British market through the Commonwealth Preference system. Yet in the succeeding decades it was to become more obvious – as more countries which were largely dependent on primary production acceded to the GATT, while at the same time agricultural protectionism in the industrialized world intensified – that this was a serious flaw in what was theoretically supposed to be a seamless web of free and fair competition woven by the GATT. For most if not all the member states thus affected were poor countries in Asia, Africa and Latin America – many of them newly independent. As such they had naturally played no part at all in formulating the rules of the GATT (nor of any of the other 'Bretton Woods' institutions) in the 1940s, when their interests had not surprisingly received scant attention from the founder nations.

(It may be noted in passing, as a striking illustration of the maxim that nations will favour free trade only when and in those sectors where they feel themselves to be strongly competitive, that the United States has latterly become an ardent champion of freer trade in agriculture, frequently pillorying both the EEC and Japan for their protectionist tendencies in this area. This development, as well as the inordinate weight of US interests in shaping the rules of international trade, are also reflected in the fact that the GATT Council has belatedly, in the mid-1980s, accepted a proposal to put agricultural trade on the agenda for its next round of discussions on trade liberalization.)

Further evidence that the industrialized nations regarded it as perfectly proper to manipulate the supposedly liberal world trading system in their favour was provided by the introduction – one could say imposition – of the Short-term and Long-term Arrangements on Cotton Textiles in 1962. Initiated by the Kennedy administration in the US and negotiated through the GATT, these were ostensibly designed to reduce the disruptive effect of the LDCs' increasing inroads into developed country textile markets by limiting the growth of their exports, on the understanding that in the longer term the bulk of productive capacity would be transferred to the LDCs. As such it could be construed as in line with the fundamental spirit of the GATT in merely seeking to provide temporary, transitional relief. However, subsequent events – including the history of the later Multi-Fibre Agreement (see Chapter 7) were to show that the developed countries were by no means willing to accept a phased rundown of their textile industries in line with their loss of competitiveness.

UNCTAD

Indeed it was the growing awareness that these less developed countries were placed at a serious disadvantage both by the rules of the GATT and by its operation in practice – to add to the handicap of a poor endowment in capital and technology – which led to their problems obtaining a more prominent place on the agenda of GATT and other international institutions from the late 1950s onwards. The resulting discussions culminated in the setting up of the United Nations Commission on Trade and Development (UNCTAD) in 1964. This body was intended to work in parallel with GATT, whose offices in Geneva it shares, to bring about changes in the structure and mechanisms of international trade which would benefit the LDCs. Yet in creating it the international community took a long step towards formally recognizing that the free trade principles embodied in the GATT were in fact unworkable.

For the *raison d'être* of UNCTAD was the perception that different countries can be at very different levels of development – to the point where the notion that all can gain equally under a regime of universal free trade is both intellectually and politically unsustainable. Consequently right from its inception UNCTAD based its strategy not on any attempt to remove those anomalies in the GATT which lent it a bias in favour of the industrialized countries – so as to achieve conditions of competition which were both 'free and fair' – but rather on attempting to introduce additional distortions of a kind better calculated to help the LDCs overcome their underdevelopment, which was seen in this context more as a socio-political problem in its own right than as an obstacle to their ability to compete in world markets. This tendency has been exemplified by two of the main planks of policy which UNCTAD has sought to have implemented throughout its years of existence:-

Commodity price stabilization.
The heavy dependence of many LDCs on exports of primary commodities for both their foreign exchange earnings and their government revenues has left them vulnerable to fluctuations in world prices, which are typically determined by the free play of supply and demand as expressed on the commodity exchanges in London and elsewhere in the industrialized world. The instability arising from these fluctuations, which can also pose problems for consumers, had already been a focus of international concern before the creation of UNCTAD. As a result a number of commodities (including sugar, cocoa, coffee and tin) had become the subject of agreements between major producer and consumer countries, to the effect that in each case an international buffer stock would be created for the purpose of stabilizing prices between agreed floor and ceiling levels – that is, by buying up surplus stocks when the free market price fell below the floor level and selling from these stocks when it rose above the ceiling. Another key feature of these agreements, it should be noted, was that they generally incorporated quotas for each of the main exporting countries. As such they constituted an attempt to cartelize the market which may be seen as a forerunner of later moves among OECD countries to cartelize national or regional markets for semi-manufactures such as steel on an *ad hoc* basis (see chapters 7 and 8). Despite the questionable success of most of these agreements in achieving any durable commodity price stability, not to mention the political conflicts which have bedevilled some, UNCTAD has long sought to generalize this approach, notably through the creation of a Common Fund (to cover a whole range of commodities) at the Fourth and Fifth UNCTAD conferences in 1976 and 1980.

Tariff preferences for LDCs.
To offset the basic handicap of the poorer countries – which in most cases include limited domestic markets as well as inadequate capital and technical resources – UNCTAD has sought to obtain preferential access for their products to the markets of the

developed countries. The high-water mark of its success in this area has been the establishment of the Generalized System of Preferences (GSP) in 1970. This provided for the progressive introduction by the developed nations of concessional (if not zero) import duties on products from the LDCs.

We are not here concerned with whether or not these policies were well designed to achieve their goal of enhancing the economic strength and well-being of the LDCs – although it is relevant to record that the apparent gains to the LDCs resulting from the implementation of the GSP have been minimal, in part because developed country tariffs have shrunk to negligible levels and continue to do so, whereas non-tariff barriers are increasing and have been used with great effect to curb LDC export gains in those areas where they are most competitive, such as agriculture, horticulture and textiles. The point is rather to note that, despite continual bland assertions of support for the principle of 'liberalization', UNCTAD was in practice dedicated to the belief that market forces needed to be manipulated and distorted in the interests of achieving a better international distribution of income and wealth.

THE OECD

Yet just as the creation of UNCTAD institutionalized the emergence of the LDCs as a distinct group with interests requiring special consideration, so the industrialized nations, at more or less the same time, signified their recognition of this duality of interest by forming themselves into their own official club, the Organization for Economic Cooperation and Development, in 1961. This body evolved from the Organization for European Economic Cooperation (OEEC), which had been set up in 1948 as a grouping of European states responsible for coordinating the administration of Marshall Aid, but which was now reconstituted to include the United States and Canada[11] and to encompass a broader range of concerns. It would be wrong to think of the OECD as a sectional pressure group, even in the limited sense that UNCTAD was an LDC pressure group (the developed countries were after all represented in UNCTAD as well). Indeed, to the extent that it was more than an informal consultative body, the main role of the

OECD was to coordinate the bilateral aid programmes of its members *vis-à-vis* the less developed countries.[12]

But although, to give credit where it is due, the OECD demonstrated a proper concern for the problems of the LDCs, there can be no doubt that its establishment also reflected the industrialized countries' perception of the need and scope for closer collaboration among themselves – in monetary as well as commercial fields. For however laudable the aims and work of the GATT may have seemed to them its inevitable tendency to move at the pace of the slowest (in other words, the most economically backward) meant that it could not adequately meet the needs of OECD members, who at that time were enjoying unprecedentedly high growth in both output and trade – principally with each other. In short the creation of the OECD amounted to a further implicit assertion – mirroring that of the LDCs behind UNCTAD – that, while theoretically all nations are equal under the GATT system, some are clearly more equal than others.

THE EEC

Another institution perhaps still more exposed to the charge of being a rich man's club is the European Economic Community. Inaugurated in 1957, its purpose was more obviously political than the OECD, since its founders saw it as providing a vehicle both for post-war reconciliation in Western Europe and for giving the member states collectively a greater degree of influence in world affairs than they could possibly have had individually. Yet however worthy these aims may have seemed in purely political terms, it cannot be denied that, as a customs union, the EEC was intended to discriminate against non-members and as such was a negation of what was originally supposed to be one of the central principles of the GATT.

It is true that Article XXIV of the GATT does provide for the creation of customs unions and free trade areas on the specious grounds of 'the desirability of increasing freedom of trade by the development, through voluntary agreements, of closer integration between the economies parties to such agreements.' This glib contradiction of the principle of non-discrimination is, however, somewhat mitigated by the proviso that any such customs union must not result in a greater degree of protection against third countries than existed previously. To the extent that the Community has ostensibly respected this condition – though only if protection is measured in terms of tariffs and other formal restraints to imports rather than NTBs – it may be said to have conformed to the letter of this rather anomalous loophole in the GATT. Yet precisely by virtue of its ability to exploit this concession – along with the exclusion of agriculture from the coverage of the Agreement – the EEC has been able to flout the spirit of the GATT without incurring any serious censure by the international community. (In fact the case of the EEC serves to highlight an important anomaly in the GATT definition of free trade, namely that the principle of non-discrimination is inherently incompatible with moves towards increased economic and political integration of countries with each other, unless such integration involves all countries to an equal degree).

As against this the EEC has tried to present itself as in the vanguard of enlightened thinking on the question of economic relations with the LDCs. Its posture on trade has been to offer progressive reduction of all tariffs on non-agricultural imports from those states associated with it under the Lomé Convention of 1975. At the same time – in what may be considered its most distinctive contribution to the pattern of development aid – it has provided a degree of automatic financial compensation to LDC exporters of certain commodities in the event of their earnings being unduly depressed by falling world prices (something which UNCTAD has unsuccessfully demanded on a much larger scale in the context of its campaign for a Common Fund).

Once again, however, these initiatives could hardly be presented as having much to do with liberalization of trade, especially as the 50 or so associate LDCs only account for some 12 per cent of the population of the less developed world (Asian and Latin American countries are excluded from participation). Moreover, even those countries which are associates have found that, as in the case of the GSP, where they are in a position to compete effectively (as, for example, in horticulture) they often find non-tariff barriers standing in their way. Indeed a fairer reflection of the EEC's record on trade liberalization in relation to the LDCs is provided by its history of entering into bilateral preferential trade agreements with countries which are excluded from the Lomé Conven-

tion – notably ones in the Mediterranean region.[13] These arrangements amount to a rejection of the GATT principle of non-
discrimination on a scale not matched by any other OECD country
or group of countries in the post-war period.

THE FACILE CONNECTION

In view of the lack of convincing evidence that the post-war system
of international trade based upon the GATT has ever even come
close to matching the definition of an open trading system in any
genuine sense, it may be thought remarkable that it has retained
such a high degree of credibility. For, as observed in the previous
chapter, there remains a quite striking measure of unanimity in the
ranks of official opinion in support of the view that free trade was
an essential element – if not *the* essential element – in the
prolonged post-war boom enjoyed by the industrialized world up
to 1973, and that its restoration is a central precondition for the
revival of prosperity. Such large-scale apparent perversity requires
some explanation. In fact it is hard to escape what is perhaps the
most obvious conclusion, namely that this view is based largely on
superficially compelling circumstantial evidence in the shape of the
rapid expansion of world trade which has characterized most of the
period since the foundation of GATT. Such growth – amounting to
over 400 per cent in real terms between 1948 and 1973 (excluding
the centrally planned economies of the Eastern bloc) – was much
faster than that achieved in any previous period for which records
exist. It is not therefore in the least surprising that many people
were only too ready to believe that the coincidence of the creation
of GATT – the first institution ever to exist for the international
promotion and regulation of free trade – with the start of an
unprecedented boom in world trade and prosperity constituted
irrefutable evidence of cause and effect: that is, that free trade did
indeed lead to prosperity.

The possibility that these twin phenomena might in fact amount
to no more than a coincidence – or rather that cause and effect
might just have been confused – seems to have occurred to very
few. That this was so, and that the former conclusion should have
appeared the more obvious, was doubtless also the result of a

strong residual faith in the teachings of classical economics, coupled with the substantial vested interest on the part of the world's major industrial and financial corporations in maintaining a trading system which was as 'free' as possible – at least from what they would have regarded as excessive government interference.

However, as already suggested, there are grounds for believing that, whatever the precise causes of the post-war boom may have been, the fact that the GATT has been acceded to by so many countries (88 by 1983), and has been able to bring about such substantial reductions in tariffs, has been made possible by the availability of tools of economic management, including the balance of payments support mechanisms of the IMF, which national governments in previous eras had been unable or unwilling to use on any scale. The origins and importance of these practices are considered in the next chapter.

NOTES

(1) Culminating in the World Economic Conference at Geneva (1927). Following the onset of the depression another such gathering was convened at Lausanne (1932) in a futile effort to stem the tide of protectionism.

(2) Generally regarded as the arch-destroyer of mercantilist ideas in his *Wealth of Nations*, first published in 1776.

(3) R.F. Harrod, *The Life of John Maynard Keynes*. London. Macmillan 1951.

(4) Cf. G. Ohlin, Trade in a non-*laissez-faire* world, in P.A. Samuelson (ed.), *International Economic Relations*. London. Macmillan 1969.

(5) Robert E. Hudec, *The GATT Legal System and World Trade Diplomacy*. New York. Praeger 1975.

(6) Cf. Melvyn B. Krauss, *The New Protectionism – The Welfare State and International Trade*. Washington. Basil Blackwell 1979.

(7) The Full Employment Act, proposed by the Truman administration, was defeated in the Senate in October 1945.

(8) Article XII states that any country may restrict trade in order 'to forestall the imminent threat of, or to stop, a serious decline in its monetary reserves'.

(9) G. Ohlin, op. cit.

(10) GATT, Report of Activities in 1980.

(11) Membership was subsequently extended from the Atlantic to the Pacific with the successive admission of Japan, Australia and New Zealand between 1964 and 1973.

(12) Its work in this area has given rise to the development in recent years of the so-called Paris Club (Paris being the location of the OECD's headquarters), which has assumed responsibility for negotiating debt rescheduling agreements for the growing number of more or less insolvent LDCs.

(13) The most far-reaching such agreements are those with the Maghreb countries, which date back to 1969 in the case of Morocco and Tunisia and to 1976 in that of Algeria.

CHAPTER 3

The Interventionist Imperative

Throughout most of the period in which the GATT has been the cornerstone of the system of international trade there has been a widespread consensus among the leading industrial nations of the Western World that there was an obligation on governments to create the conditions in which there would be the maximum possible degree of full employment. This idea was enshrined in many of the policy pronouncements issued by both national governments and international agencies around the end of World War II. Of these perhaps the most celebrated – if only because it was drafted by the closest disciples of Keynes and under his direct influence – was the British white paper of 1944, with its commitment to 'the maintenance of a high and stable level of employment after the war'.[1]

There can be little doubt that this consensus was born of the conviction that the world-wide mass unemployment resulting from the slump of the 1930s had been an important factor in creating the social conditions which made possible the rise of Fascism and thus in precipitating the war, coupled with the evidence which the war appeared incidentally to have provided that governments had it within their power, by intervening in the economy to mobilize underutilized factors of production, to eliminate unemployment almost totally. It would be wrong, however, to suggest that this idea was purely a post-war phenomenon. Indeed both the possibility and the desirability of deploying state power to minimize economic insecurity were widely accepted before the war. For a combination of the intensity and duration of the 1930s depression and the teachings of Keynes – as embodied in his *General Theory of Employment, Interest and Money* (1936) – were such as to convince a growing number of influential people that slumps could no longer be regarded simply as unavoidable but transient misfortunes. In addition the experience of Roosevelt's New Deal programme in the USA and, ironically, of pre-war Nazi Germany gave grounds for believing that such economic catastrophes were as unnecessary as they were unacceptable. 'By the end of the decade . . . there was a widespread belief that depressions could at least be partially prevented. The notion that they must be allowed to run their course was virtually extinct.'[2]

THE SOVIET CHALLENGE

An additional factor – perhaps indeed the decisive one – behind this change in attitude to state intervention in the economy was the emergence of Soviet Russia as an economic and military power on a world scale. This development was all the more striking in view of the chronic backwardness of the Russian economy prior to the revolutions of 1917 and of the upheavals to which it was subjected in the subsequent civil war which dragged on until the early 1920s. But, although the fact was perhaps little appreciated in the West before World War II, it was eventually recognized that, by mobilizing its resources under full state control, the USSR had succeeded in transforming itself from an underdeveloped, largely peasant country into a major industrial force within the space of a generation – albeit at enormous cost in terms of political repression. It had done so, moreover, during a period when the industrial economies of Western Europe and North America were, in sharp contrast, largely afflicted by depression and stagnation (table 3.1).

Table 3.1
National Income Growth in Selected Countries, 1929–37 (annual average per cent change)[3]

France	Germany	Italy	UK	Canada	USA	USSR (1927/8–37)
−2.1	+2.8	+1.9	+2.3	−0.3	+0.1	+15.5

This remarkable achievement posed an ideological and political challenge of major importance to the capitalist West, especially when after the war the Soviet Union came to be seen for the first time as an expansionist power in both Europe and Asia. For, notwithstanding the harsh and authoritarian methods involved, the Soviet system seemed – by its success in expanding its output so rapidly – to hold out the prospect of greater economic security for the individual, if not of higher material living standards, than the traditional *laissez-faire* model of capitalism. At the same time in the emerging world-wide ideological struggle between the two systems there were growing fears in the West – which lasted well into the 1960s – of being outstripped in both economic and military capability by the seemingly unstoppable juggernaut of Soviet industry. 'The two systems are now on trial in the eyes of the world to see which can enrich itself fastest, and which can use its resources more effectively in promoting the happiness and well-being of its citizens. At present growth rates, one can foresee a point on the graph at which Soviet production per head will in fact surpass ours.'[4] Although such extreme fears were subsequently to be proved groundless, there is no doubt that, as we shall see later, they inspired the relatively belated decision of the United States – for virtually the first time ever in peacetime – to engage in direct state participation in the productive sector.

THE KEYNESIAN REVOLUTION

However, in the initial post-war period, as noted earlier, the primary concern of the governments of most Western industrialized countries was to promote full employment. The principal method employed by them for this purpose was the application of what came to be known as 'demand management'. The reason for this was primarily that the Keynesian economic theories which were then ascendant identified deficient effective demand as the main cause of slumps – contrary to the teachings of traditional orthodoxy, which tended to ascribe them to excessive increases in costs and prices. The basic principle of demand management was that it sought to influence the overall level of economic activity by providing stimulus to purchasing power when output appeared to be running below capacity (as reflected in the rate of unemployment) and, conversely, applying restraint when excess demand seemed in danger of 'overheating' the economy – of which the main symptom was rising inflation.

The principal instruments of demand management were those of fiscal and monetary policy – often regarded as distinct alternatives to one another but in practice inextricably linked. Fiscal policy can be said to consist of adjustments to the balance between public expenditure and taxation, an increase in the budget deficit (or a reduction in the surplus) implying an expansionary intention, while moves towards a reduced deficit or increased surplus would be designed to have the opposite, or deflationary, effect. Monetary policy works rather by influencing the supply and price of money and credit, whether through the manipulation of interest rates or through quantitative controls on bank lending. The connection between fiscal and monetary policy results from the government's need to borrow to cover its deficits, thus affecting the overall balance of supply and demand for credit and, potentially, the level of interest rates.

Clearly there was nothing revolutionary in the notion that it was the state's responsibility both to determine the pattern of public revenue and expenditure and to control the amount of currency in circulation (if not necessarily the volume of bank credit). What was new in relation to pre-war practice in most countries was rather the idea that these instruments should be applied with a view to regulating the aggregate level of activity – that is, in pursuit of 'macroeconomic' policy objectives. Yet the fact that they had for long been almost universally[5] regarded as the proper sphere of state activity perhaps helped to ensure that no one was inclined to query the legitimacy of their use in the context of the post-war Bretton Woods system of international economic relations. Indeed it was seldom suggested that the application of fiscal and monetary policy in relation to purely domestic macroeconomic management might have a distorting impact in relation to international competitive forces. Indeed it was evidently the general opinion that if a country chose to pursue a more deflationary policy than its trading partners any competitive advantage it might thereby gain in the form of lower relative prices was simply the reasonable reward for thrift and restraint. (Although it could also be argued – and frequently has been – that excessive reliance on deflation could inflict long-term damage on a country's economy by inhibiting investment and thus innovation and productivity growth.)

However, as revealed by the discussions surrounding the 'employment clause' in relation to the ITO and the GATT, there was considerable fear from the outset among some countries that their ability to compete in an open international trading system might be compromised by the domestic policies they adopted. As observed in chapter 2, this problem was eventually dealt with in the context of the GATT by a fudging of the rules in the shape of the balance of payments escape clause, which in effect allowed countries whose external position had been undermined by their pursuit of a relatively expansionist economic policy at home to claim a temporary respite from their commitments to maintain free access for imports.

THE CONTRADICTIONS OF BRETTON WOODS

By contrast the other principal arm of the Bretton Woods system – the International Monetary Fund – in practice imposed a somewhat more rigorous discipline on member countries. This it did by requiring them to maintain fixed parities for their currencies against each other and against the US dollar (whose value was fixed in terms of gold), with devaluation or revaluation being permitted – at least in theory – only in exceptional circumstances. The implicit assumption was that these parities fairly reflected the relative competitiveness of each country's economy and that all should seek to maintain those relativities – or at least to ensure that any change should only occur as a gradual process.

Yet this precept left unanswered the crucial question of who was to be responsible for taking corrective measures in the event of a significant imbalance resulting in pressure for a change in parities. In theory the IMF rules were neutral on this point, suggesting that those countries whose external position was strengthening because of such an imbalance should be as much obliged to take remedial action – e.g. by expanding their economies faster – as those in the opposite case. In practice, however, pressure was almost invariably much stronger on the weaker economies. This tendency may seem only natural in view of the strong residual preference among international bankers for policies of fiscal and monetary restraint such as were usually associated with the stronger countries, and the inevitable propensity of speculators to put their money into the strongest currency.

It is thus not surprising that countries which tended to find themselves, because of their weak external position, subject to frequent pressure to take corrective measures – which almost invariably entailed domestic austerity – increasingly resented the discriminatory way in which the system operated. Often this was compounded by the feeling that it failed to make due allowance for peculiar structural problems which placed an undue burden on certain countries. For example, Britain, which suffered from a chronic balance of payments problem during the immediate post-war period, tended to stress the onerous requirement of sustaining sterling as a reserve currency as a reason why it should receive special consideration. Yet the resulting dissatisfaction with the system did not lead to any very serious pressure for its reform – perhaps because there was such a wide divergence of views as to what should be done, but also perhaps because even the most handicapped among the OECD countries was enjoying a spectacular rise in income and prosperity during the 1950s and 1960s and thus saw no compelling reason to rock the Bretton Woods boat. For the same reason, moreover, it was possible for countries to bend the rules of the system so as to alleviate competitive pressures on them without arousing serious resentment from their trading partners.

In fact they generally sought to avoid resorting to the escape clauses of the GATT and the IMF – which respectively permitted them, in case of demonstrable emergency, to impose temporary import controls or to devalue their currencies – since such measures offered no enduring relief in the case of a structural balance of payments problem and in any case only served to draw attention to a country's weakness. Rather they were wont to adopt the less obtrusive – if still only palliative – expedients of using the approved instruments of macroeconomic management in such a way as to favour domestic products in their own market, thus breaching the spirit of the GATT if not its letter. For instance internal taxes were often structured so as to bear more heavily on products which were predominantly imported than on competing goods which were locally produced (for example, differential excise duties on alcoholic beverages in Britain). Likewise monetary policy could be employed in a discriminatory fashion by imposing tighter consumer credit restrictions on some goods than on others – which might in some cases be seen as being as much an artificial stimulus to exports as a deterrent to imports.

Although such devices, taken in conjunction with some of the inconsistencies which were built into the GATT at an early stage, could be seen as a safety valve which prevented the Bretton Woods system from blowing apart much earlier than it did, they were not sufficient to paper over the fundamental conflicts of interest in the world economic order indefinitely. When the end came, with the removal by President Nixon of the fixed link between the dollar and gold in 1971, it was the culmination of mounting political and economic differences between the United Staes and her major West European trading partners – particularly France and West Germany. For Gaullist France had long resented what it saw as the imposition of American economic power on Europe by means of 'dollar imperialism' – by which it meant the exploitation by US-owned corporations of the reserve currency role of the dollar to acquire an undue domination of European finance and industry – while the West Germans were increasingly irritated by continual US demands for the revaluation of the Deutschmark in the interests of relieving pressure on the dollar but with consequent damage to the competitiveness of German industry.

Yet while from a Gaullist standpoint the end of the Bretton Woods system which this event signified could be viewed as marking, above all, the end of US economic hegemony, it is more appropriate to look on it as the inevitable outcome of the inherent tensions within the system. Admittedly the relative decline of US strength and authority – resulting both from the debilitating effects of the Vietnam war and from the growing economic power of the EEC and Japan – was an important factor in weakening political commitment to the Bretton Woods world order. Yet the fundamental cause of the system's collapse was the ever more obvious impossibility of containing countries with increasingly divergent economic perceptions and objectives within the strait-jacket of a fixed exchange rate regime. As such the debacle of 1971 may be seen as in a sense a vindication of the advocates of the 'employment clause' in relation to the ITO in the 1940s (see Chapter 2). At all events few would now dispute that it was the single most decisive incident in the demise of what may be termed the disciplined competitive environment of the post-war world.

THE CONSENSUS FOR MANIPULATION

To the extent that this was recognized at the time, however, it was not for the most part viewed as an undesirable development. On the contrary the general consensus among academic economists, politicians and the press was that the consequent move to 'floating' exchange rates represented an overdue relief from the burdens imposed by enforced adherence to often unrealistic fixed parities, and that this new-found freedom could only be beneficial to the formulation of soundly based economic policies.[6] Few appreciated that the abandonment of this discipline had opened the way to the more or less unbridled manipulation of exchange rates, which was often protectionist in effect if not in intent, and that the consequent tearing up of an important part of the international rules of the game was bound to be a step towards anarchy and instability. The general failure to perceive this at the time is perhaps attributable to the continuing euphoria of the 1960s' boom and the belief that continued growth was both sustainable and capable of minimizing the significance of other problems.

Yet aside from the mounting evidence of distortion of the 'natural' pattern of competition which resulted from the use of the accepted techniques of macroeconomic management, the implicit commitment of OECD governments to alleviating or preventing the ravages of economic hardship threatening those living or employed in particular regions or industries meant that they were bound to resort to more overtly selective instruments of intervention. Indeed the absolute right, if not duty, of governments to do this in case of pressing need was established very early in the development of the post-war economic order. Moreover, just as the case for Keynesian-style demand management policies was largely won before the war, so the practice of direct state intervention in and support for specific industries already had a long history in a number of OECD countries. Indeed in certain cases – of which, as we shall see later, France and Japan were the most notable examples – it was a tradition unbroken since the pre-capitalist era.

Some economists have actually tried to lend intellectual respec-
tability to the use of selective intervention and subsidy as an
alternative to tariffs, even arguing that the former were generally
preferable to the latter.[7] Whether or not their writings significantly
increased the propensity of countries to resort to non-tariff
distortions of the market, it is striking that they are largely
innocent of any serious consideration of the effect which subsidies
might have in disrupting the pattern of international trade and
thereby provoking retaliation. Indeed to the extent that this
possibility is considered at all, its danger is largely discounted on
the grounds that any country receiving the dumped exports of
another country would tend to welcome them as a benefit to its
consumers rather than as a penalty to its producers.[8] Such an
assumption is questionable on a number of grounds and in any case
has surely been demolished by the experience of the decade since
1974. One might note in passing, however, that such erroneous
theoretical conclusions are bound to result from relying on the
simplified two-country models typically used by economists in the
field of international trade. For while it may seem superficially
reasonable – if only on the basis of a short-term perspective – for
country A to regard the subsidies it receives through the dumped
exports of country B as a net benefit, it should be obvious that any
third country not in receipt of such subsidies from B and also hit by
lost export sales to A would take a rather different view. By
comparison even the authors of the GATT were hard-headed
realists.

The facility with which these contradictions were ignored or
glossed over by even the most avowed enthusiasts for *laissez-faire*
principles is illustrated by the fact that it was not in those countries
with a relatively *dirigiste* background that the concept of direct
selective intervention was first sanctified in the aftermath of war,
but in the nation most committed by instinct and custom to the
ideas of the free market – the United States. For it is clear that the
need for such direct intervention was the guiding principle behind
the so-called Marshall Plan, which was devised by the US
government and implemented between 1947 and 1952. This
programme was intended to promote the collective revival of the
war-ravaged economies of Europe (in practice it was confined to
Western Europe, since the Soviet bloc countries declined to
participate). It sought to achieve this objective through massive

transfers of financial resources to be used both for rebuilding economic infrastructure and for re-equipping and relaunching specific industries. Some $12 billion was disbursed under the Plan – 90 per cent in the form of grants and the balance as subsidized or officially guaranteed loans. Few people at the time or since have doubted its crucial role in creating the conditions both for the spectacular economic recovery of the beneficiary nations and for the overall pattern of growth and prosperity which prevailed for a generation up to the early 1970s.

Yet equally it is scarcely deniable that the Marshall Plan went far to legitimizing many of the ideas and practices which have become the hallmark of post-war interventionism and the implicit justification for the multifarious forms of market distortion which are characteristic of modern protectionism. For leaving aside the geopolitical considerations which inspired it, its central underlying assumption is that free competition in trade is only beneficial and acceptable if it takes place on terms which are not manifestly biased, to a disproportionate degree, in favour of one nation (or corporation) rather than another. In the particular case of the post-war Western industrialized world it was obvious that the European countries had either lost a large part of their basic infrastructure and industrial capacity or, as in the case of Britain, were financially crippled as a result of the war. At all events there was clearly no chance whatever of their being able to compete on equal terms with the overwhelmingly powerful US economy, which so far from being damaged by the war had been enabled to expand its productive capacity and technological sophistication to levels far beyond the reach of its trading partners. From this it followed that there was a need for positive discrimination in favour of the disadvantaged countries – a principle which, as we have noted, had already been conceded (if somewhat grudgingly) in the GATT. The important difference with the Marshall Plan is that it effectively introduced a whole new dimension of protectionism – in the shape of selective state subsidization – which was both more flexible and potentially more discriminatory than the blunt instrument of temporary direct import controls sanctioned by the GATT.

If few qualms were expressed at the precedent set by the Marshall Plan it was perhaps because the social and political factors in its favour far outweighed any considerations of equity or consistency in relation to the free market philosophy which may be said to have inspired the GATT. Moreover the very success of the project was such as to dispel any residual reservations there may have been, especially as it could be said to have corresponded to the spirit of the GATT in so far as it was only a temporary programme of aid which ceased once the beneficiary countries were strong enough to stand on their own feet. However, of the numerous imitations of the Marshall Aid model which were to follow, few were anything like as successful or, precisely for that reason, as temporary.

The problem of underdevelopment

The main targets of such subsequent aid were, of course, the less developed countries (LDCs). As already noted, the emergence of most of these countries to independence in the post-war period focused increasing attention on the problem of economic underdevelopment. In addition to taking account of this through certain clauses in the GATT[9] the Bretton Woods system provided for the channelling of development aid funds through the International Bank for Reconstruction and Development (IBRD) – better known as the World Bank – to finance projects and programmes in poorer countries.[10] Such multilateral aid has been supplemented by aid from individual developed countries, which have felt an obligation to provide it – if never on the scale or with the intensity of the Marshall Plan.

The theory of economic development and underdevelopment – on the basis of which aid to LDCs was and is justified – is the subject of a vast literature which it would be impossible to try and analyse here in any comprehensive fashion. It is fair to say, however, that the overwhelming weight of academic and official opinion in the 1950s and 1960s favoured those theories which stressed the tendency and ability of backward economies to make a dynamic response – manifested in expanding output and rising living standards – to the opportunities afforded by access to investment capital, advanced technology and open international markets. At its most naïve this view was carried to the point of suggesting that LDCs could be expected, in a more or less spontaneous manner, to emulate the pattern of development followed by Britain, Germany and the United States in the nineteenth century. Such facile optimism was confined to a small minority, however. The majority view among economists was that LDCs required, to a varying degree, a measure of assistance to enable them to reach the point where they could realize their potential for dynamic expansion according to the Western model – a potential which few doubted they possessed.[11]

This is not the place to dwell on the manifest failure of such theories to be validated in practice. Rather the important point is to note that they rested on the assumption that the economic and commercial dice were unfairly loaded against certain countries in terms of access to capital, technology and markets, and that selective intervention was justified to remedy this imbalance – just as it was thought to be in the case of the war-shattered economies of Western Europe which benefited from Marshall Aid. As we shall discover, however, once the principle of intervention was conceded, it became impossible to draw a clear and rational boundary between those market-distorting practices which were admissible and those which were not.

Security preoccupations

The pattern of economic intervention in the post-war non-Communist world which we have described thus far may be said to have corresponded to, if not been inspired by, Keynesian ideas. In other words it rested on the assumption that state intervention in the economy – whether on a macroeconomic or selective basis – was necessary as a means of correcting the perceived deficiencies of the traditional *laissez-faire* market system. In essence this perspective was largely a social one, whether applied on a national or an international scale. That is to say that it stemmed mainly from the conviction that it was not acceptable that certain social groups or, as it was perceived in the case of the LDCs, certain entire nations should be condemned to long-term economic deprivation because of the malfunctioning of the free market system.

Yet it is hardly surprising that this justification for government intervention in the economic sphere was soon extended to encompass other reasons of state which were seen as equally compelling, particularly those relating to national security. Of course the state's role in the maintenance of national defence is one which pre-dates by far the Industrial Revolution – and its acceptance may even be said to coincide with the decline of feudalism. Moreover the extent to which this idea was entrenched and to which, accordingly, defence procurement was seen as an aspect of the economy which could not be governed by normal market factors, is recognized in the GATT, which specifically exempts armaments and other products connected with state security from the rules applying to trade in general. At the same time the potential importance of government actions in the field of military expenditure in determining the level of activity in key sectors of the economy (e.g. shipbuilding) was widely appreciated before World War II. Conversely, and most important of all, the positive correlation between the level of a nation's industrial and economic power on the one hand and its actual or potential military strength was an article of faith which transcended ideology.

The full significance of this fact in the post-war world was brought home to the West, once again, by the seemingly inexorable advance of the Soviet Union. For whereas at the end of World War II the USSR was clearly well behind the USA in military-related technology, it was obvious by the mid-1950s that it had largely remedied the deficiency – particularly in relation to nuclear weapons. The danger that it might actually overtake the West in this area was not, however, widely recognized until the sensational Soviet advance into space technology with the launch of the first sputnik in 1957 and the first manned orbit of the earth by Yuri Gagarin in 1961. This development came as a profound shock to the United States, where there had hitherto been a certain tendency to disparage the Soviet capability for independent technological advance. Not only was the launch of the Sputnik a heavy blow to US ideological self-confidence and belief in the functional superiority of their economic system.

'Few nations have seen so many of their basic assumptions shattered so swiftly as the Americans have in the weeks since Mr Khruschev propelled his first sputnik into space. In quick succession, they have been made to realize that their technicians are not in every possible respect the most efficient in the world, that their education system has some dangerous flaws and that soon they will no longer be able to protect their homeland against nuclear attack'.[12]

This made them appreciate the need for a collective effort – unprecedented in the US in peacetime – to meet the threat of an actual Soviet military superiority, which was clearly implied by their success in space (indicating as it did a formidable capacity for launching long-range ballistic missiles). Indeed this development appeared to be a clear vindication of those such as Professor Galbraith who had been arguing that the unaided operation of the market mechanism was inadequate to ensure the most desirable allocation of resources – from the public point of view – in the US or any other economy.

> 'Private enterprise did not get us atomic energy. It has shown relatively slight interest in its development for power for the reason that it could not clearly be fitted into commercial patterns of cost and profit. Though no one doubts the vigour with which it addresses itself to travel within the United States, General Motors has little interest in travel through space'.[13]

The United States was not slow to demonstrate that it had learnt the lesson. The establishment of the National Aeronautics and Space Administration by President Kennedy in 1961, with the specific goal of placing a man on the moon by the end of the decade, was the start of a determined effort to show that the Western economic system could not merely equal but surpass that of the East in technological achievement, and at the same time to ensure that Soviet technology could not pose any threat to Western security. What was hardly commented upon at the time, however, was the fact that this policy decision represented a commitment by the world's foremost exponent of the free market system to undertake as much public expenditure as was necessary to gain and keep a lead in key areas of advanced technology, in the national interest. Moreover the case for doing so was clearly accepted virtually unanimously by American opinion – not perhaps because it perceived any close connection between a US presence in outer space and military security as such, but simply as a matter of national and political prestige.

It is apparent that by its exertions in the field of aerospace over the last 20 years the United States has succeeded in its aim of establishing a clear lead over the Soviet Union in the related areas of technology and has thereby also enhanced its international prestige and military security (even if, ironically, its relative economic and political power *vis-à-vis* the rest of the world has declined at the same time). Yet it has also served to illustrate the importance of the two-way interaction between state procurement programmes with a primarily military or strategic purpose and the level of technological competence of industry and thus of national competitiveness in certain sectors of trade. For the space programme has made a major contribution to the development of technology in the field of integrated circuits (microprocessors), which has in turn helped to assure a US lead in this and the related field of computer technology. In addition it has made possible important breakthroughs in metallurgy and telecommunications (satellites), among other fields. Thus the US space programme – which cost American taxpayers over $100 billion in its first ten years – may be seen at one level as the most expensive single research and development programme ever undertaken anywhere, although not one on which the adequacy of the return on the investment will ever be, or could ever have been, determined.

THE CORPORATIST TRADITION

Just as strategic considerations – in the broadest sense of the term – have led successive US administrations to distort what would otherwise have been the market-determined pattern of investment in certain fields of research and development, so other countries have done likewise – though usually with rather less emphasis on strictly military factors. Indeed, while US intervention in this form has in the post-war era been more conspicuous and on a much bigger scale than that of other OECD countries, some of the latter have a much longer history of direct state support for both research and investment in industry.

France
Among European countries France has perhaps the longest unbroken tradition of state involvement with private enterprise. Indeed from the time of Colbert in the seventeenth Century the French have never wholly abandoned the mercantilist practice – which in Britain fell victim to the liberalizing ideas of Adam Smith

– of trying to promote commercial and industrial expansion by the granting of privileges or monopolies to certain companies or individuals. This evolved after World War I into the setting up of companies owned jointly by the state and private interests (*sociétés d'économie mixte*) and, after World War II, into a structure of economic planning in which the private sector's investment plans were coordinated with and partly financed by the state.[14]

Japan

A similar corporatist approach to economic organization has also been characteristic of Japan from the time of its opening to the West, which dates from the so-called Meiji Restoration in 1868. This event precipitated an intensive effort by the new regime to modernize the Japanese economy along Western lines, involving the creation of numerous industrial enterprises by the state. These were eventually transferred, as an act of political patronage, to large private conglomerates (the *zaibatsu*) which, in return for their privileged position, took care to act in conformity with the wishes of the government – something they may be said to have done ever since.[15] In addition, since World War II the government, through the Ministry of International Trade and Industry (MITI), has played a central role in promoting and coordinating investment, though the scale of direct government subsidies to either research and development or actual investment has been relatively small compared with some European countries. Instead the most distinctive and successful tool of state intervention in Japan has been the banking system, which has been subject to government domination and manipulation to a degree quite unknown in other OECD countries. This has been achieved by the effective right of veto over private banks' credit policies which is exercised by the Bank of Japan, on which the whole financial sector is dependent for funds.[16] At the same time, by itself extending loans to particular companies or industries, the Japan Development Bank has usually been able to induce the private banks to unlock much larger funds for the same purpose on the tacit understanding that the government will effectively underwrite any loans.

In both the French and (especially) the Japanese cases the motivation for such intervention has in the post-war period had little to do with preoccupations over defence. Rather it stemmed in each case from a desire to ensure the country's independent technological and industrial capability, although it is debateable how far this was out of concern for guaranteeing domestic prosperity and social harmony or rather based on more traditional nationalist considerations. Yet in the final analysis this question is perhaps of purely academic significance, since apart from the somewhat indecisive attempts to codify in the GATT the justifications for interference by national governments with freedom of trade, no international agency – still less any national government – has attempted to formulate a universally applicable set of rules governing the circumstances in which state intervention in the economy is admissible. For what ultimately counts is whether, in the judgment of the government concerned, intervention is desirable in the national interest – or, as may often be a more accurate definition, in its own narrower political interest.

There can at all events be little dispute that by the mid-1960s at the latest it was generally accepted that governments were entitled to intervene in the economy for reasons other than the simple need to avert recession or prevent a rise in unemployment – problems which in any case most people by then believed had been largely conquered.[17] Indeed one of the most influential books of the period castigated the governments of Western Europe for their failure to coordinate their assistance to and planning of industry so as to be better able to resist the competition of the giant US multinationals, which were – the author claimed – far more effectively assisted by their government.[18] Indeed, as we shall show in the next chapter, the pressures have been mounting in recent years to use the state's power to distort market forces precisely in order to maintain or increase the international competitiveness of particular industries in individual countries. The general chorus of enthusiasm for this approach effectively drowned the few voices which were raised in warning that it was tending to undermine the basic assumptions of the competitive model of international trade.

One such voice in the early 1970s was that of the distinguished economist Professor Harry G. Johnson, who vigorously condemned this trend towards indiscriminate intervention and 'the new mercantilism'.[19] As we have suggested, however, the phenomenon could not justly be regarded as new in the sense that it amounted to a revival of a long-dormant approach to economic organization.

For the truth is that in Europe and Japan at least basic mercantilist attitudes had never been wholly suppressed, even if in some countries their influence had fluctuated over the years. If there was a new element in its resurgence in the 1960s it was perhaps that the United States – a country whose struggle for independence had been in large measure a protest against the tyranny of traditional mercantilism – was now in effect embracing the doctrine with unprecedented enthusiasm.

NOTES

(1) *Employment Policy*. Cmnd 6527. HMSO 1944.

(2) J.K. Galbraith, *The Affluent Society*. Harmondsworth. Penguin 1962.

(3) Derived from data in (1) J. Cornwall, *Modern Capitalism – Its Growth and Transformation*. London. Mcmillan 1978; (2) A. Nove, *An Economic History of the USSR*. Harmondsworth. Penguin 1969.

(4) M. Shanks, *The Stagnant Society*. Harmondsworth, Penguin 1961.

(5) A distinguished exception to this rule has long been Professor F.A. von Hayek, who continues to maintain that currency issue should be a competitive business involving the private sector (cf. *The Denationalization of Money: An Analysis of the Theory and Practice of Concurrent Currencies*. London. Institute of Economic Affairs 1976).

(6) Cf. *The Economist*, 18 December 1971.

(7) Cf. J.E. Meade, *The Theory of International Economic Policy, Volume II: Trade and Welfare*. Oxford University Press 1955; W.M. Corden, *Trade Policy and Economic Welfare*. Oxford University Press 1974.

(8) W.M. Corden, op. cit.

(9) Notably Article XVIII, which permitted the protection of 'infant industries' in LDCs.

(10) Established at the same time as the IMF in 1944, a major aspect of the IBRD's role was originally seen – as its name implies – as being to assist in the transition to a peacetime economy.

(11) Cf. W.W. Rostow, *The Stages of Economic Growth*. Cambridge University Press 1960. The notion, advanced in this work, that LDCs could be expected, in the foreseeable future, to reach a point in their development at which growth would become self-sustaining demonstrated what now seems a remarkable faith in (1) the ability

and willingness of backward societies to adopt rapidly the attitudes and practices of the industralized West, and (2) the possibility that growth could long remain self-sustaining in any economy, developed or otherwise.

(12) *The Economist*, 14 December 1957.

(13) J.K. Galbraith, *The Affluent Society*. Harmondsworth. Penguin 1962. Chapter 25.

(14) A. Shonfield, *Modern Capitalism*. Oxford University Press 1965.

(15) Richard Storry, *A History of Modern Japan*. Harmondsworth. Penguin 1968. Chapter 5.

(16) G.C. Allen, *Japan's Economic Policy*. London. Macmillan 1980.

(17) M. Shanks, op. cit., page 31.

(18) J-J Servan Schreiber, *The American Challenge*. London. Hamish Hamilton 1968. The author at no point indicates any awareness of a possible fundamental conflict between the approach he urges and the principles of free market competition.

(19) H.G. Johnson, Mercantilism: past, present and future, in H.G. Johnson (ed.), *The New Mercantilism*. Oxford. Basil Blackwell 1974.

CHAPTER 4

The Changing Nature of Competition

The two preceding chapters, taken together, have served to highlight what has been a widely noted paradox in the evolution of the post-war world market economy, namely that 'there is... a sharp contrast between the trend towards liberalization in economic relations and the tendency towards more extensive government intervention in domestic economic affairs'.[1] Yet it would be quite wrong to conclude that these two apparently conflicting developments have merely had the effect of cancelling each other out, and that the pattern of international exchange has therefore been determined in much the same way as in previous phases of the capitalist epoch.

THE GATT AND THE RISE OF THE MULTINATIONALS

In fact the removal of formal barriers to trade promoted by the GATT and, perhaps even more, the easing or ending of currency exchange controls did create unprecedented scope for the largely uncontrolled movement of goods, services and capital across frontiers. Even though, as has already been remarked, this liberalization was from the outset heavily qualified by the retention on the part of national governments of the ability to suspend or circumvent their commitment to free trade, the practical impact of these reserve powers in the 1950s and 1960s was not sufficient to prevent either a dramatic growth in world trade or an ever increasing integration of world markets. The most striking manifestation of this apparent trend towards a global economy was undoubtedly the emergence of what came to be known as multinational or transnational companies.

As with other features of the post-war world economy which are often thought of as innovations peculiar to the present era – such as state intervention in industry – multinational companies are by no means a new phenomenon. Leaving aside the traditional colonial trading companies dating from before the Industrial Revolution – which arguably are not wholly analogous to modern multinationals because the basis of their activities was primarily commercial, with productive activities being undertaken only to the extent that they were necessary to sustain the flow of trade – the establishment of overseas manufacturing subsidiaries by major industrial companies was already common practice before World War II. However, before the war it was fairly obvious that the only justificationfor setting up such foreign outposts was to gain access to the specific national market in which each was located – and which would otherwise often have been rendered largely inaccessible on account of high tariff barriers. By contrast since the war multinationals have been in a position to treat their various subsidiaries as specialized parts of a more or less fully integrated global operation, making it possible for each national market to be supplied from one or more of a number of group establishments – whether located within the country concerned or elsewhere – in accordance with considerations of profit maximization.

The ability of multinationals to pursue such global strategies under the centralized control of their head offices was not, it should be stressed, solely a function of the relaxation of formal barriers to trade and the freer convertibility of currencies which were instituted under the Bretton Woods system. A factor which could be seen as being of equally decisive importance was the enormous advance in the speed of international communications – in the shape of both air transport and telecommunications – while improvements in the methods of data processing based on computer technology made the centralized monitoring and appraisal of foreign subsidiaries' management possible as never before.

Yet if the factors which made it legally and physically possible to manage multinationals as integrated global operations can clearly be regarded as distinctive developments of the post-war period, the basic motivation for companies to develop an international dimension was on the whole more traditional. For it had long been a commonplace that any company operating exclusively in a national market was bound, as long as it remained profitable and expanding, to come up against the eventual constraint of demand which, if not actually saturated, was growing too slowly to absorb the output which could be achieved by expanding capacity on the minimum scale necessary. This problem tended to arise even earlier in those countries such as the USA where the laws against monopoly were relatively strictly enforced. Companies faced with such obstacles to their expansion at home were therefore compelled to look abroad for new investment outlets.[2]

This inherent outward urge was arguably intensified in the post-war era by the increasing resort of governments to the interventionist practices referred to in chapter 3. The use of monetary and fiscal policy – particularly when it involved changes in credit restrictions or indirect tax rates – was often a source of frustration to industrial companies, who saw these moves as disrupting their sales projections and thus reducing the confidence they required to justify new investment. Ironically such government moves to restrict the growth of domestic demand were often justified on the grounds that they gave companies an incentive to seek greater export sales, and indeed this hope was often fulfilled in those countries, notably West Germany and Japan, where foreign investment by national companies was either not traditional or even officially frowned upon. In the Anglo-Saxon countries, by contrast, and to an increasing extent elsewhere, such interference with the normal working of the market by national governments was unquestionably an irritant from which companies sought to escape by expanding their operations in other countries. For even if such policy gyrations were common to virtually all OECD countries it was logical to suppose that, by spreading production across a number of different national centres, companies could even out their overall sales and profits figures and thus achieve greater predictability.

Multinationals bypass government policies

Moreover, thanks to the liberalizing impact of the Bretton Woods system on international trade and payments it was increasingly possible for companies to bypass or neutralize the effect of measures taken by governments in pursuit of what were generally seen as legitimate national economic policy objectives. Nowhere was this capability more marked than in the field of monetary policy and credit expansion. For the general adoption of more or less full convertibility of their currencies by most OECD countries after 1958 led almost inevitably to the development of credit creating mechanisms which were beyond the control of national governments and which neither the IMF nor any other suprana-tional body was empowered to supervise. This was because the resulting freedom of financial movement between one country or currency area and another made possible the creation of 'offshore' banking institutions based on non-resident deposits. In the abs-ence of effective regulation these organizations were increasingly able to extend credit more or less indiscriminately to companies (or governments) in all parts of the world. [3] Likewise multination-als were correspondingly enabled to circumvent government monetary policy in one country by borrowing in another. A particularly striking instance of this was the response by major US companies to the Johnson administration's imposition of quantita-tive restrictions on domestic credit expansion in 1968. For the prinicipal result of this move was to ensure that the business was diverted to overseas banks operating in the so-called Eurocurrency markets – many of them subsidiaries of US banks – while the impact on the overall level of US credit growth was negligible. [4]

Examples could be multiplied of the ways in which multination-als have managed to circumvent or frustrate the policies of national governments – and indeed are the subject of a copious literature. For our purposes it is sufficient to note that the combined effect of the Bretton Woods based liberalization of international exchange and payments and the increasingly interventionist stance of national governments was to create a form of international 'macroeconomy', though one in which there was a total absence of central responsibility for regulation of the economic aggregates such as existed at national level. The ability of the multinationals to exploit this power vacuum in ways which might be contrary to the public interest was, from the late 1960s, a subject of increasing concern to a wide range of political opinion. For, as one of the earlier writers on the subject pointed out, even if one could suspend disbelief long enough to accept that what was good for General Motors was good for America, 'one must stretch the imagination to believe that the interests of General Motors, or any other company, could invariably be the same as those of the US...and all the other countries where it operates'. [5]

This concern was all the greater in view of the size and growth of the larger multinationals in relation to that of many of the countries where they operated. For the annual turnover of several of these companies was greater than the gross domestic product of the smaller OECD countries and far in excess of that of most less developed countries,[6] while at the same time it was authoritatively forecast – on the basis of an extrapolation of their rapid rate of expansion up to the early 1970s – that by the end of the century some 200 multinationals would account for the bulk of industrial output in the world's market economies.[7] This last point incidentally underlines the fact that anti-trust restrictions were another important area of government control which could be largely evaded by firms operating in an international context.

In view of all the evidence of the growing power and independence of the multinationals it was not implausible to claim, as many informed observers did, that they constituted a threat to the sovereignty of nation states.[8] If this belief has lost some credibility in the last few years it is not because governments or international agencies have taken any steps to curb their growth or privileges, but more probably because the prolonged recession which set in after 1973 has shown that multinationals are unable either to avert or fully to protect themselves from fundamental world-wide economic trends. Indeed a number of them have proved to be just as vulnerable to the downturn as most LDCs – as demonstrated by the apparent insolvency of such famous names as Chrysler, International Harvester and Massey Ferguson (among others). In these circumstances the companies concerned have often been compelled to turn to governments for aid – aid which has almost invariably been forthcoming in view of the official perception that a formal bankruptcy of any company of this size would have damaging implications for other sectors of the national economy – not least the financial sector – as well as for social indicators such as unemployment.

INTERDEPENDENCE OF MULTINATIONAL AND GOVERNMENTS

Thus what these setbacks have revealed is that, despite their apparently basic conflicts of interest, multinationals and governments ultimately depend on each other, and indeed have always done so. For both have to survive in a rapidly changing and unstable world economy which neither can control but from which equally neither has the option of retreating into a narrow protected cocoon. In the case of multinationals the reason for this is rather obvious, in so far as by definition they must continue to operate on a world scale. For governments the options appear on the face of it to be slightly greater, since the possibility of operating some form of siege economy undoubtedly exists for many, particularly those with relatively abundant natural resources – assuming that obligations under the GATT and the IMF are not regarded as sacrosanct. However, while the short-term attractions of such a policy may appear considerable – as they did to many governments before the war – it has long been apparent that no industrialized country could long sustain such a posture without seeing a marked decline in the living standards of its people as well as the loss of any claim it might have had to political or economic significance in the world.

In the final analysis, therefore, the relationship between multi-nationals and national governments is far too complex to be summarized in any glib slogan. For while their basic interests remain sharply at variance they also have areas of common interest – particularly in times of world-wide recession. This is particularly noticeable in relation to questions of international trade. For however much there may be differences as to such factors as the location of production and tax levels, multinationals and govern-ments find themselves increasingly at one in seeking to neutralize international market forces.

We have already seen in the previous two chapters why governments, although theoretically opposed to monopolistic tendencies and usually having a nominal responsibility for curbing anti-competitive practices, in reality often have their own compell-ing reasons for not wishing to expose their industries to the full force of international competition. In the case of corporate interests this preference should come as no surprise, in spite of the rhetorical support which big business has frequently lent to the principle of free trade. For, as economists from Adam Smith to Galbraith have pointed out, entrepreneurs who are loud in enthusiasm for the general principle often find that in their own particular case it is not appropriate to apply it too rigorously, if at all. This is of course because the primary goal of any company under capitalism is always the maximization of profit – whether in the short or the long run – whereas free competition has a tendency to diminish profits. Hence the historical propensity of established enterprises to seek to eliminate competition, along with other sources of uncertainty, and to achieve the maximum degree of monopoly.

As we have seen, multinationals have found considerable freedom under the Bretton Woods system to develop, if not monopolistic, then at least oligopolistic control of world markets, thanks to the absence of any kind of international anti-trust control system. This in turn has enabled them to make what is arguably their most striking, even if least publicized, contribution to the development of world trading patterns since the war, namely the practice of intra-company trading across international frontiers. While statistical data on this phenomenon are extremely scarce, it is probably reasonable to estimate that, on average, well over 40 per cent of all the exports and imports effected by multinationals are transfers between subsidiaries of the same group and thus virtually by definition immune to any genuine competitive pressure. Appreciation of this fact is, of course, quite devastating for those who seek to uphold the neo-classical model of the determination of trade patterns – that is, the one implicit in the GATT – as well as for those who would attribute the great post-war boom in international commerce to the existence of an 'open' trading system. These ideological concerns, however, were of little importance to governments as long as the net effects of such intra-company trading on their national balance of payments was not consistently negative and thus remained compatible with overall economic growth and prosperity.

MARKET FORCES UNTAMED

One school of thought at least has seen in these tendencies the emergence of an all-powerful corporatist alliance between big government and big business, in which competition is effectively eliminated except among the less powerful economic agents outside the 'planning system'.[9] Yet such a conclusion would appear to be a considerable over-simplification, as the onset of recession has once again underlined. For it is clear that, contrary to the widespread and understandable optimism of the 1960s, the corporatist mechanisms identified by Professor Galbraith – significant though they are – are not capable of indefinitely manipulating markets so as to achieve the degree of stability or predictability which both governments and large companies are seeking.

This may be explained partly in terms of the exhaustion of the Keynesian model of macroeconomic management evident in the recession itself. This is reflected in the fact that it is no longer possible artificially to boost demand to levels sufficient to assure full employment – largely because of the progressively higher levels of inflation which this process has entailed. In addition, however, it is to be explained by the failure to make the international corporatist power structure either cohesive or all-embracing enough to prevent uncontrollable outbreaks of competition – a danger which, as will be shown in later chapters, was further increased as the recession threw the leadership of the international market economy into increasing disarray.

The main inherent source of this weakness was perhaps the same profit-seeking tendency which we have argued leads capitalist entrepreneurs to prefer protection and oligopoly to free competition. For despite this preference there are always some elements, even among the large established companies which form part of the Galbraithian 'technostructure', who will seek to exploit an opportunity to boost their profits – even if this is likely to be at the expense of other members of the charmed circle. Their propensity to do this will naturally be all the greater to the extent that they perceive that there are significant actual or potential sources of competition which have not been, or indeed cannot be, neutralized by oligopolistic pressures.

The technology treadmill

One such destabilizing factor which ensured that even the largest multinational companies could never remain wholly at ease with regard to competition was the inexorable advance of technology. Although no satisfactory measure of the speed of change in this area has been or probably can be devised, few would perhaps quarrel with the assertion that the past 40 years have witnessed an acceleration without precedent since the Industrial Revolution. For private sector companies this has been a mixed blessing, since they have an inherent ambivalence regarding advances in technology, as they have towards competition itself. This stems from their need to maximize returns from both existing and new investments, a goal that can be threatened by technological change which, if it is too rapid, can render plant obsolete even before the initial outlay has been recovered.

Such dangers were largely discounted in Galbraith's model of the new industrial state, according to which the financial power of the dominant companies meant that they alone could afford to finance the research and development necessary to ensure technological leadership, while they also had the market power to retain control of it – through their role as dominant suppliers of the market as well as through the patent system and licensing.[10] Yet even to the extent that this description was a fair reflection of reality it still entailed an element of instability in that the requirement to spend large sums on research and development so as to retain market dominance also implied the need to maintain a steady rate of investment to produce a return on the R & D, thus making technological change a self-fulfilling prophecy – while at the same time it imposed an ever increasing burden on corporate finances.[11] In short the pursuit of technical innovation was a competitive treadmill from which it was impossible for large companies to escape, even if – as increasingly occurred – the state could often be induced to bear a major share of the cost.

Indeed the increasing tendency of governments to subsidize or wholly finance not only R & D programmes but actual productive investments – for reasons which were often quite at variance either with the aims of multinationals or with the apparent dictates of market forces – was another important and unpredictable source of market disruption which forced even the largest private sector companies to maintain their competitive vigilance. For, as we have observed, direct state intervention in industry – either for narrowly strategic reasons or out of consideration for broader economic objectives – was by the 1960s a universally accepted tool of national policy. Yet because no mechanism existed, or was even thought desirable, for coordinating the industrial support strategies of different national governments – let alone for relating them to the global strategies of multinationals – such interventionism was inevitably a source of uncertainty as to the supply/demand balance of world industrial markets. Thus the efforts of governments to guarantee the security and stability of domestic industry by directly participating in it themselves were, contrariwise, a disruptive influence at the international level – a paradox which can be recognized as more apparent than real once one appreciates that such subsidization strategies are basically a form of mercantilist protectionism.

It was not only through its rapid rate of change that technology imposed new competitive strains on the world market economy from the 1950s onwards. Another of its more burdensome aspects was often the sheer scale of investment – in productive capacity as well as research and development – which any company or country with serious pretensions to be an independent force in the market needed to undertake if it was to maintain its position. In consequence it became increasingly common to find that industrial enterprises, whether in the public or the private sector, needed to obtain a share of the world market considerably in excess of that which was available in their domestic market alone if they were to achieve anything approaching an acceptable rate of return on capital.[12] For established multinationals this need to achieve such 'economies of scale' in output in order to ensure competitiveness was in many respects a source of strength, since it tended to protect their oligopolistic position against potential new entrants to the industry who lacked their ready access to a wide range of national markets. But precisely for this reason national governments which perceived their domestic industries to be threatened by this combination of the awesome power of the multinationals (usually foreign owned) and rapidly advancing technology felt compelled to try and secure a sufficient share of world markets for their own nationally based enterprises.

To achieve this it was obviously insufficient to think in terms of giving national companies protection in the home market alone, while it was clearly not practicable – except perhaps in the insignificant markets of the residual colonial empires – to obtain exclusive or preferential access to overseas markets in an era of supposedly non-discriminatory trade.[13] In short, for any country seeking to secure or maintain a position for itself at the forefront of technological and industrial progress, the traditional methods of protectionism were as irrelevant to their objective as they were inimical to the principles of the GATT. In view of this, it was inevitable that governments in this predicament should choose the path of subsidizing indigenous enterprises – whether in the private or public sectors[14] – and, where appropriate, helping them to expand into the multinational sphere.

NEW COMPETITORS FOR THE MULTINATIONALS

This compulsion to subsidize locally controlled enterprises was not confined to those countries, mainly in Western Europe, which were anxious to have an independent capability in advanced technology. It also extended to many of the countries outside the OECD – including a number which could be defined as LDCs – which felt the need to industrialize as a way of securing both their independence and the benefits of modernization and higher living standards. These countries were also, by virtue of their less developed status, allowed more latitude in protecting 'infant industries' under the terms of the GATT. As such they did not necessarily fit very easily into the multinationals' world-wide empires unless they either adopted an aggressively welcoming attitude to foreign investors (like, for example, Singapore) or had a relatively large domestic market (as in the case of Brazil). A substantial majority of the LDCs did not fall into either category, and among these a small but growing minority – including South Korea, Taiwan and India – pursued, with varying degrees of determination, a policy of industrialization based largely on local enterprises and capital. Moreover, for reasons which will be discussed in the next chapter, such enterprises were often of necessity under effective state control.

Newly industrialized countries
The membership of this group of 'newly industrialized countries' (NICs) was given a considerable boost after the oil price explosion of 1973, when a number of oil-exporting nations began to use their newly acquired wealth to create an industrial base against the day when their petroleum reserves would be exhausted. Indeed, as we shall see later, the same event had a significant indirect impact in expanding the industrial capacity of LDCs in general – a process which occurred largely at the behest of the international banks, which were then seeking to 'recycle' the vast quantities of surplus OPEC cash for which there were at that time few borrowers in the

industrialized countries. This development naturally served to create still more poles of instability from the point of view of the multinationals – and also, incidentally, demonstrated a divergence of interest between themselves and the international banks – since most of the new Third World industrial enterprise supported by this lending was outside the control of multinationals and indeed posed an obvious threat to their market dominance.

Japan

Of all the world's market economies which have failed to be incorporated in the 'planning system' of the multinationals, far and away the most important is Japan. The reason for this is that, although it had long ceased to be thought of as a less developed country, after World War II it had succeeded – on a variety of historical and political grounds – in having itself classified as something of a special case among developed countries. Thus it was permitted, for a long time after the war, to retain relatively high tariffs and what amounted to a prohibition on foreign investment – a fact which largely explains its failure to join the OECD until 1964. Even after that date permission for foreign companies to invest in Japan was given very sparingly, and usually only on condition that such investment took the form of a joint venture with a local firm.

This exclusion of Japan from the mainstream 'multinational economy' might not have had such crucial importance but for the country's subsequent emergence as the world's second largest industrial power, with unmatched competitiveness in many areas of the most advanced technology as well more traditional industries. As it was, by the mid-1970s it had achieved, or was well on the way to doing so, world dominance in such manufacturing sectors as shipbuilding, motor vehicles, consumer electronics and photographic equipment. It had done so, moreover, without the benefit not only of foreign investment in Japan but of more than minimal Japanese investment in other countries.[15] Thus non-Japanese multinationals – i.e. nearly all of them – were forced to respond to the emergence of this formidable rival by sharpening up their own competitiveness rather than by seeking to neutralize it by means of takeover and absorption.

Centrally planned economies

Another source of unpredictable and uncontrollable competition which has been of increasing significance, even though it remains much less of a threat to Western multinational enterprise than Japan, is constituted by the centrally planned economies of the Soviet bloc and China. Since these countries' economies had been set on a path of development in isolation from the market economies it was obvious that Western multinationals would have little opportunity of investing in them, even if they wished to do so. What was less obvious for a long time was that these countries might have reason to try and expand their own share of Western markets, particularly as they felt a growing need for hard currency to purchase Western products and technology. The latter trend was given a particular impetus by the efforts of Western countries – commencing with West German Chancellor Brandt's so-called *Ostpolitik* in the early 1970s – to seek new markets in the Soviet bloc, an initiative which received the enthusiastic backing of many multinationals.

This approach met a ready response from the Comecon countries, but their need to achieve a matching increase in their sales to the OECD countries in order to pay for these sophisticated imports was a snag whose implications were little appreciated in the West until later. Thus multinationals, in their eagerness to obtain turnkey contracts for the supply of (for example) petrochemical plant to Comecon countries, were prepared to agree to 'buy-back' arrangements by which they undertook to accept a portion of the output of these complexes – which in any case could seldom be absorbed by the local market in the short term – in part payment. The destabilizing impact of such deals on Western markets was subsequently compounded by the increasingly frantic efforts of some Comecon countries to solve the problem of their soaring indebtedness to the West by boosting their exports to hard currency areas – often at prices which demonstrably amounted to dumping in terms of the GATT (of which in any case hardly any of them were signatories).

The same problem was rather quicker to reveal itself when the People's Republic of China began likewise to open its doors to the West in the mid-1970s. A bonanza similar to the Comecon one was widely anticipated in the OECD countries until it was made known that the Chinese authorities were reluctant to purchase high technology and capital equipment on credit, and moreover were seeking to pay for them in the currency of traditional Chinese exports. The thought of finding themselves with millions of tons of unwanted pigmeat and textiles on their hands was enough to cause a rapid cooling of enthusiasm among Western companies and governments for this new departure in East-West trade. None the less both Chinese industrial capability and their exports of manufactures to the market economies have continued to expand and thus to constitute a further source of uncertainty in relation to the attempts of multinationals to bring a measure of order and stability to the world-wide markets they serve.

TRADE NEITHER FREE NOR CONTROLLED

In summary, the overall pattern of international competition which has unfolded in the last 30 years corresponds neither to the romantic *laissez-faire* myth of free market success nor yet to the picture, so beloved of many on the Left, of an all-powerful monopolistic conspiracy of multinationals. Thus, while it is difficult to sustain the view that international exchange has in essence been any more 'free' than in earlier epochs, it is equally clear that competitive pressures were far from having been neutralized. What was distinctive about the post-war period was that, instead of the distortion of competition being effected by formal tariffs and quotas, it was the result of efforts by the various power blocs concerned – usually operating in isolation from each other – to use the increasing number of policy instruments at their disposal to alter the competitive odds in their favour. In this context the multinationals should properly be seen – particularly in view of their size and financial strength in comparison to that of many nation states – as constituting simply additional participants in the global power struggle, whose interests were just as likely to conflict with each other as with those of governments.

Yet the necessity for the various interested parties to deploy and extend these techniques of what has been termed 'policy competition',[16] in order to attain the vital goal of securing access to export markets, may prove to have sown the seeds of much greater instability than occurred as a result of earlier bouts of trade conflict, such as that of the 1930s. For before World War II it was feasible for at least some countries to withdraw into almost total economic isolation – especially if they had colonial empires to add to their domestic markets – and stabilize their economies independently, even if this meant a sharp drop in living standards.[17] By now, however, not only have these captive colonial markets vanished, to be replaced by new sources of mercantilist competition in the shape of independent Third World countries; the degree to which national economies have become locked into a position of mutual interdependence – as a result of 30 years of rapid expansion by the multinationals and of the increasingly inescapable need for economies of scale in manufacturing – is such that a reversion to economic separate development seems virtually inconceivable for industrialized countries. But if there is evidently no turning back it must equally be wondered whether present practices and trends can be allowed to continue without the whole pattern of international trade degenerating into a morass of competitive distortions of the market, with potentially explosive consequences – political as well as economic.

NOTES

(1) G. Ohlin, Trade in a non-*laissez-faire* world, in P.A. Samuelson (ed.), *International Economic Relations*. London. Macmillan 1969.

(2) They could also, it is true, diversify into new product markets, although such a strategy – as many modern 'conglomerates' could testify – can be fraught with management problems.

(3) Quite apart from its effects on aggregate monetary growth this development led to a gradual erosion of the prudential standards of the banking industry as governments shrank from imposing orthodox reserve ratios on banks for fear that they would transfer their operations to more free-wheeling financial centres, many of which – such as the Bahamas or Liechtenstein – deliberately sought to encourage such activities.

(4) P. Einzig, *Parallel Money Markets. Volume I: The New Markets in London*. London. Macmillan 1971.

(5) C. Tugendhat, *The Multinationals*. London. Eyre and Spottiswodde 1971.

(6) Cf. C. Tugendhat, op. cit.

(7) J.H. Dunning, The multinational enterprise, *Lloyds Bank Review*, July 1970.

(8) R. Murray, The internationalization of capital and the nation state, in H. Radice (ed.), *International Firms and Imperialism*. Harmondsworth. Penguin 1974.

(9) J.K. Galbraith, *The New Industrial State*. London. Hamish Hamilton 1967.

(10) J.K. Galbraith, op. cit.

(11) Thus, for example, The British Pharmaceutical industry – according to a report presented to the National Economic Development Office in 1981 – had seen an average fourfold rise in real terms between 1969 and 1980 in the total cost of developing a new drug.

(12) It should be stressed that this applied not only to high technology industries but (perhaps even more) to mature industries such as motor vehicles where the technology was not necessarily especially advanced but required frequent heavy outlays – for example, on tooling up for new models.

(13) Cf. H.G. Johnson, Mercantilism: past, present and future, in H.G. Johnson (ed.), *The New Mercantilism*. Oxford. Basil Blackwell 1974.

(14) The fact that an increasing number of such enterprises were state owned or controlled naturally made it all the easier to disguise the extent of subsidization.

(15) The enormous concentration of financial and industrial power which Japanese corporations could none the less bring to bear on their conquest of world markets – quite apart from the strong backing they received from the government – is indicated by the fact that in 1980 *each* of Japan's four largest conglomerate *zaibatsu* (Mitsubishi, Sumitomo, Dai-ichi Kangyo Bank and Mitsui) had an annual turnover greater than that of the largest Western multinational (Exxon).

(16) B. Belassa, in R. Amacher *et al.*, *Challenges to a Liberal International Economic Order*. New York. Columbia University Press 1980.

(17) It did not, of course, prevent increasing international friction – and indeed exacerbated it to the extent that it inevitably tended to foster nationalist sentiment.

CHAPTER 5

The Instruments of Intervention I: Subsidies to Investment and Production

To appreciate adequately the range and impact of the neo-protectionist measures referred to thus far and the extent to which they have become ingrained in the economic fabric of the industrialized market economies in the period since World War II, it is necessary to dwell on them in rather more detail.

The least obtrusive of these interventionist weapons were naturally those which took the form of aid or subsidies targeted specifically at the production process rather than those which impinged directly on export or import transactions. Yet for reasons which should be obvious they were just as much a form of protectionism as the latter and in the present context should therefore be considered as being just as important. None the less, to the extent that such aids could more readily be presented as having some kind of social purpose rather than a narrowly protectionist one it is perhaps useful to consider the two types of policy tool under separate headings. This chapter consequently confines itself to those measures concerned with subsidizing the investment and operating costs of industrial enterprises, while those involving more direct distortions of trade flows are examined in chapter 6.

INCENTIVES TO PRIVATE INVESTMENT

It would be hard to find a country in which the market economy plays a significant role where the government (almost regardless of its proclaimed political ideology) does not consider private productive investment to be generally desirable. If asked to justify this view most would probably cite – or would have done until quite recently – the beneficial effects on the level of employment which it induces both directly and indirectly through 'multiplier' effects in the rest of the economy. A subsidiary reason, although one which has latterly assumed more prominence, is the need to modernize the economy on the basis of advanced technology, something which obviously implies the need for new investment – public or private – and often seems to call in particular for investment by foreign-owned companies. Such foreign investment, it is widely believed, tends to bring with it the benefit of 'technology transfer'. This argument – which can be seen as a strategic one in that it reflects a desire to avoid too great a degree of technological dependence on overseas sources – is one which is bound to receive more emphasis as the case for promoting investment on employment grounds begins to look questionable. For it is increasingly apparent that the traditional belief – much cherished in Britain by Keynesian economists and trade union leaders – that there is a strong positive correlation between the growth of investment and that of employment has been invalidated by a surge in technological change so powerful that labour productivity has risen steadily even in the recession, something which many previously thought virtually impossible. However, as a lot of trade unionists have come to recognize, even if they must now regard investment as a destroyer rather than a creator of jobs, as long as economic prosperity is seen to depend on a competitive struggle for world markets based on technological leadership, their own countries have no choice but to enter the fray.

Tax concessions

Governmental efforts to stimulate or attract such investment take a variety of different forms. Of these the most basic – and more or less universally practised – is that of tax concessions. In most countries virtually any investment in fixed assets, other than real estate, qualifies for an automatic allowance against company taxation, while in some instances a government may even go as far as offering new investors from abroad a total tax holiday for a number of years, often regardless of the level of investment involved. In addition it is common to find, especially in less developed countries, that customs duties are waived on inputs which the company concerned can show need to be imported, while it is also possible to obtain fiscal favours from local authorities, which provide another dimension to the competition between governments for investment and jobs. In the United States, indeed, it is the states rather than the federal government which typically offer the most lavish tax concessions to investing companies, often giving discriminatory tax advantages to individual companies. A notorious example of this was the deal whereby the government of Pennsylvania induced Volkswagen to locate their US assembly plant in the state, involving a five-year exemption from property tax and the treatment of the plant site as a foreign trade zone, as a result of which the finished vehicles attracted lower duties.

For a number of reasons, however, tax concessions alone tend to be a less than adequate means of promoting private investment. From the point of view of governments they can often prove rather a blunt instrument, since – despite the above evidence to the contrary from certain American states – it is generally felt that considerations of equity (if not the law) require that they be applied in an ostensibly even-handed manner. Consequently, if a government wishes to provide an incentive to private investment or participation in a particular project it can only use tax concessions to this end if it offers similar advantages to other companies undertaking investments – particularly those operating in the same industry. This tends to apply less in LDCs, where a private company (typically foreign owned) investing in a manufacturing industry will often expect to have a virtual monopoly of the local market for the product because of the limited scale of local demand. It is thus possible in such countries to offer tax concessions either on a one-off basis or exclusively to foreign companies operating in specific sectors without arousing any objection from local firms. In industrialized countries, by contrast, companies which might respond to such inducements often have compretitiors who are liable to insist on equal treatment. A well-publicized instance of this arose in Britain in 1982, when the government attempted to offer what would have been discriminatory tax relief on chemical feedstocks to Exxon and Shell in order to induce the companies to proceed with a joint investment in a petrochemical plant. On hearing of this proposed secret deal BP successfully demanded parity of treatment.

From a company point of view there is another reason why tax concessions are often less attractive than other forms of subsidy, especially if they are in the form of relief on direct tax liability (i.e. on profits). This is the fact that the benefits are not realized immediately in terms of group cash flow, and not until the project has broken even (often some years later, if at all), if the company has no profits from other operations in the country concerned against which to offset its initial capital expenditure. By contrast more direct subsidies, such as grants or cheap loan finance, have an immediate beneficial impact on corporate cash flow independently of when (if ever) the project itself breaks even. Thus concessions in the form of direct tax relief can be relatively expensive for governments and less attractive to companies than direct cash subsidies.

Consequently governments have increasingly tended to see selective incentives to investment as the most cost-effective way of securing the desired objective. In fact selective subsidy of private sector investment is, once again, by no means a novel practice, even outside those countries, such as France and Japan, with a long-standing tradition of state support for private business. In particular the availability of subsidised loan finance has been widespread, particularly in continental Europe, throughout the post-war period. Indeed such mechanisms for aiding industry could be said to have become an entrenched part of the European approach to economic management from the time of the Marshall Plan, which made great use of concessional loans in its programme of industrial regeneration.

Subsidized credit

Soft loans – that is, at subsidized rates of interest – and loan guarantees have been available in virtually all European countries to industrial ventures of every kind, though with particular emphasis on small businesses and projects located in the more deprived areas. Perhaps the most striking single example of this tendency is Italy, where by 1978 no less than 76.5 per cent of outstanding industrial borrowing had been advanced under the government's *credito agevolato* system of low interest loans. Even in Britain, where by contrast with other European countries it has always been possible to tap the more developed equity market for a much greater proportion of private investment capital, competitive pressures – compounded by those of the recession – have in recent years obliged governments to offer more incentives of this kind, notably in the shape of the Thatcher government's Loan Guarantee Scheme for small businesses.[1]

We have already referred to the far-reaching importance of the Bank of Japan's role in providing *de facto* guarantees to private bank loans to industry, while the enduring tight restrictions on the domestic credit market have tended to ensure that interest rates remain low in comparison to those prevailing in other countries. In the United States, where ideological objections to such state intervention tend to be more outspoken, government assistance to private investment has none the less been appreciable. Thus successive governments have provided grant aid – through the Economic Development Administration – to companies investing or expanding in the more deprived areas of the country, while loan guarantees to small enterprises have long been an established part of the US scene. In addition the federal government has also been forced to succumb at various times to pressures for assistance to very much larger companies. However, this has usually been accorded not by way of providing a stimulus to new investment but rather in cases where a corporate collapse has threatened either a major financial crisis or serious social consequences or both – as in the case of the Nixon administartion's underwritng of loans outstanding to the bankrupt Penn Central Corpoation in 1970 and President Carter's similar action in support of the deeply troubled Chrysler Corporation in 1979.

Lenders of last resort

Indeed US experience points to a yet more fundamental way in which state power has been used to underwrite the finances of the corporate sector throughout the capitalist world in the post-war period. This has come about by the assumption by central banks of the role of 'lenders of last resort' to the banking industry. This too has been a gradual process whose history dates from before World War II and may perhaps be said to have its origin in the banking catastrophe which coincided with the onset of the Great Depression in 1929-31. To prevent this upheaval from turning into a global financial holocaust acceptance credits and other instruments held by British and US banks on bankrupt financial institutions in Germany and other Central European countries were effectively taken over by the Bank of England and the Federal Reserve and subsequently written off over a period of years. Within the United States, where bank failures had wrought particular havoc in the domestic economy, one of the earliest acts of the Roosevelt administration in 1933 was to enact compulsory insurance of bank deposits through the newly created Federal Deposit Insurance Corporation (FDIC). Yet it was obvious from the outset that this institution would not be able to pay out on more than a fraction of insured deposits in the event of a major banking crisis, and indeed an additional line of credit from the Treasury has always been available to bail it out should the need arise. In fact in 1982 it was observed that the FDIC's reserve fund of $11 billion amounted to little more than 1 per cent of insured deposits, while the Treasury line of credit was officially stated to be for no more than $3 billion, and that consequently many economists believed that the government would give limitless support in case of necessity[2] – a point fully borne out by the response to the Continental Illinois Bank collapse in 1984.

It is not of course to be expected that central banks or governments will make it explicit that they will intervene to shore up the markets in all cases of a threatened major industrial or financial failure. However, there is undoubtedly a widespread implicit belief that under modern capitalism governments simply cannot accept that the full force of marketplace logic – in the shape of outright bankruptcy – be brought to bear on major industrial or financial companies which get into difficulties, and that this belief has conditioned the attitudes of many banks in their pursuit of business. This fact, combined with the progressive relaxation, under competitive pressures, of the prudential standards imposed on banks through minimum liquidity or equity ratios, led to an explosive growth of bank lending in the 1960s and early 1970s, in which, in the words of one leading bank executive (speaking in 1973), 'lots of people...are not considering risk at all; it's pure money rental.'[3] While it would obviously be wrong to attribute all the excesses of the banking industry to official acquiescence in its profligacy, there undeniably was and is a sense in which many of the bigger loans to the private sector – not to mention those to LDCs and other sovereign borrowers – were thought of as being backed by an unwritten official guarantee. This impression was strengthened by events in Britain in 1973-74, when the collapse of the property and shipping boom brought overnight ruin to a number of 'fringe' banking organizations. Faced with the real prospect that the crisis would even bring down the mighty National Westminster Bank – the second largest in the country – the government and the Bank of England moved swiftly to launch a 'lifeboat' into which the survivors of this financial shipwreck were expeditiously hauled with no expense spared. In thus coming to the rescue of property speculators it could plausibly be argued that the government was signalling its willingness to do the same for any firm or group whose collapse would pose a big enough threat to the whole system.

Direct grants

Such intertwining of the interests of governments and private big business is also manifest in more direct forms of investment subsidy. Although outright grants are seldom available automatically in respect of new investment – and then only on a limited scale in most cases – the discretionary use of grants is a weapon at the disposal of most OECD governments and one which is particularly vital in the competition for 'footloose' investment by multinationals. Although it is frequently denied that such competitive bidding between governments occurs – still more that the multinationals actually solicit it – both common sense and available evidence indicate the contrary. Among OECD countries the phenomenon is particularly marked in the EEC, where ten governments vie with each other to secure industrial projects which have access to the whole Common Market.

Not surprisingly, detailed and comprehensive figures relating to the nature and extent of this phenomenon are not readily available. The tip of the iceberg is periodically revealed, however, when squabbling between governments breaks out into the open (as it has done increasingly in the EEC) or when a government gets itself into a position where it has invested so much political capital in securing a particular investment that public attention becomes focused on the price it has paid for doing so. Two particularly striking instances of the latter case in Britain concerned investments by foreign companies in the motor industry – a sector which still apparently holds a peculiar political attraction as a means of employment creation.

The first example was the massive engine plant which Ford decided in 1978 to locate at Bridgend in South Wales. They only did so, however, after exhaustive consideration of sites in other European countries and, needless to say, the associated inducements offered by each prospective host government. The choice of Bridgend – which was close to an area where unemployment had recently been boosted by a rundown in the steel industry – was made after overt campaigning in its favour by the then Prime Minister, James Callaghan, whose parliamentary constituency was also located in the vicinity. The decisive factor, however, was undoubtedly the package of subsidies, amounting to nearly £100 million – or over half the total fixed investment cost of the project – which the government saw fit to offer the company. Such open-handedness to a profitable multinational was all the more striking in view of the fact that Britain was at the time supposed to be applying a policy of austerity and public expenditure cutbacks under the tutelage of the IMF. A subsidy of similar size was also agreed much more recently (in 1984) as part of a deal with Nissan to open an assembly plant in the North of England (its first in Europe), although in this instance the inducement was not offered in competition with other European countries but rather to overcome the Japanese company's reluctance to undertake any manufacture in Europe at all. (This agreement, of which the details have still to be finalized at the time of writing, is a remarkable measure of the lengths to which even a relatively *laissez-faire* government such as Mrs Thatcher's is prepared to go in order to secure a politically eye-catching investment from abroad, especially as the proportion of local value added in the cars produced will be low by European standards and the numbers initially employed will consequently be low – at only 500.)

Equity participation

While the type of subsidies referred to in the examples just cited were, in effect, outright gifts, governments frequently chose to support investment projects by means of equity participation. This approach, which may be regarded as half way between a loan and a grant, can imply various possible purposes on the part of the government concerned. In LDCs, where this form of state involvement is particularly common, it is often a legal requirement that there be some form of state shareholding – even if only a minority one – in any investment by a foreign-owned company. Yet while this condition is usually imposed for political reasons it often has attractions for foreign investors, since it has the simultaneous effect of reducing their own financial outlay on any investment project and of ensuring government commitment to the project. The general approval of, if not preference for, this type of arrangement is demonstrated by the fact that there are only a handful of multinationals – most notably the Bata Shoe Co. and IBM – which refuse on principle to accept less than 100 per cent ownership of their subsidiaries. Likewise one of the most success-ful of the newly industrialized countries, Singapore, has built a reputation as an attractive location for investment by multination-als, with a dynamic, market-oriented economy, in spite (or perhaps because) of the state's ubiquitous presence as a sharehol-der in all major enterprises, which makes it – according to one authoritative source – 'the most important entrepreneur in the Singapore economy'.[4]

In more developed countries state equity participation in investment projects tends not to be undertaken for purely political reasons, although it may sometimes be viewed with more suspicion by the private corporate sector than would be the case in many LDCs precisely because the government is less likely to see its shareholding as largely symbolic and more likely to have the resources and expertise to take an active part in management. None the less many companies also see equity participation by the state as reassuring for much the same reasons as they do in LDCs. This is all the more true in those countries where the private equity market is poorly developed and where the state's involvement can ease the way to obtaining loan finance.

Italy is once again the classic example of this approach to investment promotion. Its main instrument in pursuit of it has been the Istituto per la Ricostruzione Industriale (IRI). This organiza-tion, which is yet another throwback to the pre-war era, having been established by Mussolini in 1933, is a state holding company charged with sustaining and expanding the country's industrial capability. Contrary to the position in most LDCs it tends to exercise a *de facto* controlling interest in most of the companies in which it has shareholdings, even where its stake is a minority one. For this reason its attractiveness as a partner is confined to national companies rather than foreign ones investing in Italy, even though it does not always exercise very tight control over its subsidiaries. Indeed it is fair to see IRI's role as being less that of a provider of incentives to private investment and more that of a substitute for or a supplement to the private sector where the latter appears unable on its own to fulfil the perceived need for investment in certain sectors or geographic regions.

In this context an important function of IRI – and of its sister holding company ENI (Ente Nazionale Idrocarburi) – has been to promote the rationalization of the corporate structure of the country's main industries by providing financial assistance in support of necessary company mergers in the private sector. It was that aspect of its work which initially most inspired imitation in other European countries. In Britain the short-lived Industrial Reorganization Corporation (IRC), created by the Wilson government in 1966, acted as a catalyst for large-scale mergers in the heavy electrical and motor industries (among others), while in France President Pompidou's government established the Institut de Développement Industriel in 1970 – at the very moment when in Britain the IRC was being abolished by the incoming Heath administration – with a similar purpose. With the return of a Labour government in Britain in 1974 a further variant of the IRI model was instituted in the shape of the National Enterprise Board, which was closer to the holding company concept but with particular emphasis on supporting projects in areas of advanced technology such as microelectronics and biotechnology, even going as far as to set up new companies from scratch, as well as rescuing existing private firms in these sectors – notably ICL and Ferranti – which had got into financial difficulties. It is incidentally worth noting that, although the Thatcher administration came to power in 1979 committed to abolishing the NEB, it has had to content itself with disposing of some of its assets and changing its name (to the British Technology Group) – another tacit betrayal of its professed free market ideology which has been forced on it by a recognition of modern corporatist reality.

Nationalization and complete state control of enterprises
In such ways the boundary between giving encouragement to private sector investment and direct state participation in the productive sector has become gradually blurred. Viewed in this

context the ultimate degree of state participation, namely full nationalization or the creation of industrial companies which are fully state owned from the outset, can be seen as more often an expedient designed to further traditional mercantilist aims rather than a principled act based on socialist ideology. At another level nationalization clearly does provide artificial stimulus to the private sector in so far as it enables key sectors of the economy to operate at subcommercial levels of profitability. For this permits them both to supply inputs to the private sector at what amount to subsidized prices, and to provide a market outlet for the production of the private sector in circumstances where normal market criteria would have indicated that their operations should have been severely curtailed, if not completely terminated. Thus IRI's portfolio of around 140 wholly or partly owned companies (employing some 500,000 people) has consistently made aggregate annual losses running at well over $1 billion for several years now and by 1982 had accumulated debts equal to over $20 billion. Likewise in Britain the state-owned British Steel, British Leyland and British Shipbuilders have recorded losses totalling several billions of pounds in recent years with little sign that even the present Conservative government has any serious intention of closing enough of their capacity to make them profitable in the foreseeable future, while in France the election of a Socialist government in 1981 conveniently permitted many virtually bankrupt private sector firms – including the steel companies Sacilor and Usinor, and the chemical groups Rhone-Poulenc and Pechiney Ugine Kuhlmann – to collapse into the arms of the state.

In macroeconomic terms such unprofitable operations of the nationalized sector clearly need to be considered as an extension of government fiscal policy, since they serve to limit the impact of recession both from the social point of view and from that of private industrial and financial companies, many of which would otherwise see a much more drastic deterioration in their performance and face a more tangible threat of bankruptcy. Equally it enables many sectors to obtain business in export markets when they would be quite unable to do so if they were obliged to charge genuinely remunerative prices.

It is important to note in this context that a large proportion of the industrial enterprises established in LDCs in the last 20 years have been publicly owned from the start. In addition to the factors already cited in relation to the industrialized countries, there is another particularly compelling reason – which is peculiar to LDCs – why this should be so. This is the almost total lack in most LDCs of indigenous private capital on the scale required to develop other than the smallest and least sophisticated of industries. In these circumstances there is frequently little alternative to industrialization through public sector enterprise – all the more so in conditions of world-wide recession in which the participation of multinational companies, even if it is politically acceptable, is increasingly hard to obtain.

This world-wide trend towards direct participation in industry by governments – often motivated by non-commercial considerations – helps to explain why, after several years of recession in world markets for such manufactures as steel and shipbuilding there still remains a substantial degree of overcapacity. In such circumstances it is not surprising that the private sector companies they compete with, notably in the United States, complain vociferously at such 'unfair' competition.

R & D support

Yet, as many Europeans are quick to riposte to this kind of charge, the United States has its own more or less concealed methods of subsidizing the investment costs of its industries so as to give an artificial boost to their competitiveness. Of these a particular American speciality is the field of research and development expenditure (much of which is linked to defence and aerospace procurement). No less than $47 billion of federal government money is currently spent annually on R & D – equal to some 1.5 per cent of the US national product and over 100 times more than the British government's total R & D budget for 1982-83 (whereas US GDP is only about six times the UK figure), while total French government spending in this area is said to be equal to that of the Massachusetts Institute of Technology alone.[5] Moreover, in addition to having a budget of such a vastly different order of magnitude to its European competitors, the numerous American state-funded research institutes have developed, often in conjunction with the universities, what amounts to an organic relationship with the private corporate sector, facilitating the efficient translation of research results into marketable products.

Although Europe is not at the moment a serious contender with the United States in terms of its collective research and development effort, the same cannot be said of Japan. According to *International Business Week* total civilian R & D outlays in Japan amounted to $26 billion in 1981 (there is no Japanese military R & D work to speak of) – exactly half the comparable figure for the US. If US outlays in the military field are included the ratio of total R & D spending as between the two countries is roughly 3:1 in favour of the US – or proportionately about the same bearing in mind the size of the two economies. The difference is that a very small proportion of the total Japanese figure is spent directly by the government – amounting, it would appear, to even less in absolute terms than the R & D budgets of some European countries. Yet as in the case of the promotion of actual productive investment in Japan – of which more later – the government's role as a paternalistic orchestrator of the economy gives it the ability to ensure that the R & D programmes of private sector companies are both of minimal cost to the latter and of maximum cost-effectiveness to all concerned. For not only does the state provide financial incentives to companies – in the shape of tax concessions and outright grants – to undertake R & D in approved fields, it ensures that the programmes of different companies operating in the same field are coordinated with each other and with related work at universities. Furthermore, in order to remove any corporate inhibitions over such collaboration, arrangements of this kind are formally excluded from the scope of the Anti-Monopoly Law.[6] Not content with thus effectively matching the US effort in assisting R & D programmes, the Japanese government goes further by operating a world-wide information gathering service on developments in high technology, with the collected data being made available to national companies and thus helping to keep them in the forefront of technology.

Japan incorporated

But if Japan has shown itself to be an astute imitator of the West in the fostering of technological innovation, its method of mobilizing its economic forces to fulfil what are in essence classically mercantilist objectives appear to be uniquely Japanese – though they are increasingly mirrored in the economic policies of the culturally kindred South Koreans. It is scarcely feasible in the present context, nor indeed within the author's sphere of competence, to attempt any serious analysis of the social and cultural mechanisms which enable this approach to function as effectively as it clearly does. Yet the readily available evidence would suggest that it depends on a combination of state patronage and legal authority which has been able to secure corporate compliance and cooperation in the pursuit of national economic and commercial goals. This makes it possible, for example, to induce private sector financial institutions to purchase government bonds carrying a negligible rate of interest in order to finance the country's enormous budget deficit at a manageable cost. Similarly, when it comes to promoting productive investment by the private sector, the system of 'administrative guidance' – under which the Ministry of International Trade and Industry can issue directives to companies which have the force of law – gives Japan many of the characteristics of a centrally planned economy, even though, in remarkable contrast to Western Europe as well as the Soviet bloc, the ownership of enterprises is seldom vested in the state. In the words of a well-known American analyst of the post-war Japanese economic achievement, 'the basic driving power was a result of the effective utilization of state power, of state financial organization, of state funding and of the mobilization of other state-owned or controlled resources.'[7]

Thus, while Japanese economic organization may not be as monolithic as the cliché description 'Japan incorporated' implies, it can hardly be disputed that it has gone further in the direction of establishing a comprehensive and coherent industrial policy than any other OECD country. Yet the concept of a national industrial policy or strategy is far from being unique to Japan, although in the case of the majority of OECD countries it can for once be truthfully said that this phenomenon is peculiar to the post-war era. Moreover, just as the Japanese system of administrative guidance may be seen as market distorting in so far as it implicitly underwrites a given strategy of an industrial company, so similar – if less thoroughgoing – commitments by the governments of other countries may be regarded as tending towards protectionism, in that they create a climate of confidence for investment that might well not be warranted by the market conditions which would be likely to prevail in the absence of such policy pronouncements or 'indicative planning'.

Indeed whatever may be the criteria used to determine the

choice of sectoral targets for government support, a demonstration – based on a realistic assessment of the national industry's potential world market share and of prospective costs and prices – rial Strategy in the mid-1970s many of the sector working parties, rate of return seldom appears to be one of them. Thus during the period of the British Labour government's much vaunted Industrial Strategy in the late 1970s many of the sector working parties, charged by the tripartite[8] National Economic Development Council with identifying those types of product within each manufacturing sector with the greatest potential for growth, concentrated their analysis on the scope for increasing output at minimum cost without any serious regard to the world market profile each would be facing. While this omission might seem understandable in view of the difficulties of predicting long-term trends in world markets in today's increasingly volatile economic conditions, the fact that the possibility of this being an obstacle to such plans was scarcely even raised is an indication of the degree to which wishful thinking too often becomes a substitute for hard-headed, objective analysis in formulating such industrial policies.

Similar conditioned optimism may perhaps be said to have lain behind the recent decision of four major European governments (of Britain, France, West Germany and Spain) to give financial backing to the development of the A-320 airliner to be produced by the Airbus Industrie consortium. It is true that this has been based on an apparently objective appraisal of the market prospects. However, as was conspicuously demonstrated by the British government's desperate but finally unsuccessful attempt to avoid having to provide any subsidy, the newly denationalized British Aerospace was insufficiently convinced of its potential profitability – bearing in mind the enormous risks involved and the past failure of such projects to make money – to raise the money by borrowing at commercial rates of interest.

Regional policy
Arguably the most irrational of all the manifestations of official resistance to market forces – for all its socially creditable motives – is the approach to regional policy adopted by many OECD governments, notably the United States, where (as noted earlier) the individual states have traditionally played a bigger role in providing incentives for private investment than has the federal

government. Indeed the scale of confusion and self-defeating competition is all the greater because local authorities as well as national governments can and do influence the overall pattern of policy on regional development, often without there being any mechanism for coordination of the different regions' promotional efforts either with each other or (if such exist) with the national government's industrial or regional strategies. The chaotic consequences of this fragmentation are well illustrated in Britain by the plethora of press advertisements extolling the merits – and financial incentives – offered by different local authorities from different parts of the country. The confusion is undoubtedly exacerbated within the EEC by the role of the Commission in distributing aid through the European Regional Development Fund. Yet perhaps the most telling question raised by this widespread practice of discrimination and distortion of cost factors as between regions is whether governments which lack faith in the virtues of free trade even within their own frontiers can seriously be expected to espouse it in an international context.

Perhaps the greatest irony of this situation is that practices of the kind referred to are effectively encouraged by many of those international agencies – such as the OECD, IMF, UNCTAD and the ILO – which are among the most vocal protagonists of free trade. This they do by frequently advocating the restructuring of the economies of industrialized countries – utilizing appropriate means of 'adjustment assistance' – so as to reduce their capacity in those industries, such as textiles and leather goods, in which the LDCs tend to have a comparative advantage – and transfer the workforce made redundant by this process to new 'sunrise' industries. To that extent the idea of industrial policy – and by extension many of the subsidizing tendencies which flow from it – has been given the official seal of approval at the highest international level. Yet the contradictions inherent in effectively encouraging the world-wide adoption of this approach – when no machinery for coordinating the industrial policies of different countries exists – are scarcely perceived.

DIRECT SUBSIDIES TO PRODUCTION COSTS AND REVENUES

It will be readily apparent that any attempt to distinguish, for analytical purposes, between incentives or subsidies to investment and those to production is somewhat artificial in so far as anything which boosts profitability can be seen as an incentive to investment. However, the distinction seems none the less worth making in that it serves to emphasize the fact that state subsidization of industry is not just about stimulating investment in strategic or potentially expanding sectors of the economy, but about shielding declining industries in uneconomic locations from the harsh logic of market forces.

For such direct cost subsidies are usually aimed primarily at 'sunset' industries, which are either based on outmoded and uncompetitive technology or else located in regions where the operating cost structure has been rendered uneconomic, often because of changes in the pattern and techniques of transportation. They are rather less important, at least in theory, in relation to those industries – usually ones in the newer, high technology, capital intensive category – where assistance tends to be crucial at the start-up stage, when investment costs are high and market prospects often problematic, but where profitability appears reasonably assured once these initial hurdles have been successfully overcome (assuming also that location is not a crucial factor in relation to the overall cost structure).

Discriminatory government procurement
An obvious exception to this rule, however, is what may well be regarded as the most widespread and convenient of subsidy mechanisms, namely government procurement of goods and services. The most conspicuous application of subsidy through procurement has been in the military field. Because of its connection with national security it has long been accepted that military procurement cannot be conducted on the basis of free international competition – a point which is even enshrined in the GATT.[9] At the same time it is a field where product development and manufacture is obviously heavily dependent upon the application of the most advanced technology. For these two reasons companies which are suppliers of other than the least sophisticated

military hardware are usually disinclined to undertake the necessary development and investment costs unless the government – which is generally their only customer – agrees in advance to financial arrangements which will virtually guarantee them an adequate rate of return. For their part governments which do not wish to depend on imported material, and are thus forced to go out to, at best, limited tender are reluctant to underwrite the investment costs of different potential domestic suppliers – a procedure which is clearly bound to entail multiplying the cost to the taxpayer – simply in order to maintain the appearance of competition.

Equally, governments are anxious to offset the often heavy but unavoidable budgetary burden to the maximum extent possible by seeking non-military applications with which to capitalize on the research and development costs incurred in defence programmes. The companies which benefit from this 'spin-off' thus enjoy a *de facto* subsidy – whether or not they have been directly involved in the original military contract – in so far as they are enabled to exploit for civilian commercial use plant or technology whose investment costs have been largely if not wholly written off under a state procurement programme. In this way areas of economic activity which must unavoidably be insulated from market forces tend to impinge on sectors which are normally part of the open market – and would do so even if governments did not actively seek to bring this about.

The repercussions of such cross-subsidization in terms of international competitiveness are often considerable. For instance the ability of the US aerospace industry to use R & D funded under military programmes to obtain cost advantages in civil aircraft and aero engine manufacture has contributed greatly to its near-monopoly of this market internationally. Perhaps the most striking illustration of this phenomenon is the fact that the most commercially successful jet airliner ever built – the Boeing 707 – was originally developed as the KC 135 in-flight refuelling tanker for the US Air Force. Likewise the phenomenally expensive programmes of the National Aeronautics and Space Administration (NASA)[10] – which, although not specifically military in its objectives, has obvious strategic implications and is an agency of the Department of Defense – have been instrumental in giving the United States and US-based companies a dominant position in those high-technology industries which are set to form the basis of what has been billed as the 'second industrial revolution'. In particular it has helped US industry to develop a significant lead in such vital areas as satellite communications and numerous applications of computer and laser technology.

Not surprisingly other countries have not been willing passively to watch the American 'military-industrial complex' use its state-backed financial muscle to acquire a monopoly of the most advanced technological know-how. We have already remarked on the determination of the Japanese government to match the scale of the US effort in civilian R & D (Japan has hitherto lacked, perhaps fortunately for itself, the opportunity to write off these costs under defence expenditure). In Europe, governments have used the patronage they exercise through their very large (by US and Japanese standards) public sectors as to some extent a counterweight to the cost-subsidy benefit derived by US industry from military procurement.

Thus for example successive governments in both Britain and France have effectively compelled their state-owned airlines to buy passenger aircraft manufactured by their national aerospace industries (including the financially disastrous Concorde) as part of their effort – referred to earlier – to maintain a national capability in this sector.[11] Likewise the same two countries have tended, where possible, to give preference to their main national suppliers of computer hardware – ICL and CII-Honeywell Bull – in allocating orders for such equipment on behalf of government departments and public corporations, much to the fury of major US suppliers, whose much more effective subsidization is achieved, as just noted, by other means. Similarly all countries which retain a capability in the telecommunications equipment industry give *de facto* preference to their national suppliers over foreign ones – although in the US this is not achieved by state procurement as such since the telephone utilities are in the private sector.

Such protection through procurement is not necessarily just for the purpose of assuring the survival of a domestic supplier for the national market. Indeed, as was suggested in the last chapter, given the need for high technology industries such as telecommunications equipment to achieve a substantial share of the world market – in order to amortize the vast investment cost entailed in sustaining them – such a parochial strategy is in many cases clearly not viable. Where this is so the role of state procurement in the home market is a dual one of being a marketing tool – that is, to demonstrate the functional efficiency or attractiveness of the products in use[12] – and at the same time providing a means of cross-subsidizing export sales by applying a premium price to public sector purchases at home. This form of de facto dumping is, moreover, not confined to those high technology sectors where the need to achieve economies of scale puts such a premium on exporting a substantial proportion of output; nor yet is it restricted to OECD countries. Thus it has recently been alleged that Hyundai Construction of South Korea – a subsidiary of one of that country's largest conglomerates – has been able to obtain some major civil engineering contracts in the Middle East by virtue of the fact that the heavily weighted prices attached to public sector contracts at home have enabled it to cross-subsidize export work.[13]

Subsidization of inputs

It is not only by acquiescence in the effective overpricing of public sector contracts that governments help to boost the operating profits of private sector companies. For in addition to acting to increase the latter's revenues artificially through procurement, governments can and do subsidize the costs of their inputs. We have already referred to the use of exemption from or abatement of taxes as an investment incentive – particularly in economically disadvantaged regions. More insidious, perhaps, are the subsidies given through the distorted pricing of public utility services to industry. This may be done either by holding down the level of these prices across the board or by fixing the tariff structure in such a way that domestic consumers effectively subsidize industrial ones. The first course was most openly pursued by the Heath government in Britain in the early 1970s, mainly in the interests of keeping down the general level of inflation. It none the less obviously had an impact on the competitiveness of British industry *vis-à-vis* its trading partners, although because of the mounting inflationary pressures elsewhere in the economy at that time the impact of this hidden subsidy was scarcely noticeable – except in the accounts of British Gas and the Electricity Council.

In fact, as in the case of tax concessions, subsidies of this kind are really only cost-effective when they are applied on a selective basis. This point was clearly recognized by the Dutch government following the first 'oil shock' of 1973, which resulted in massive increases in the price of all types of fuel. Conscious of the impact this was likely to have on the horticultural industry – which is of major importance to the Dutch economy but extremely energy intensive – it was quick to introduce a subsidy on fuel costs specific to this sector. This move provoked a mixture of protest and imitation on the part of the industry's European competitors, although in view of the massive subsidies and protection already extended to agriculture within the EEC this relatively modest handout to the kindred horticultural sector might not have been thought to be particularly unnatural.

An example of a much more far-reaching form of sectoral subsidization in the Netherlands is provided by the case of the country's ports, among which Rotterdam has been able to grow to become the world's largest in terms of traffic handled thanks in no small measure to the generosity of the government in assuming the burden of many of its operating costs. The port corporation is thus absolved from paying these charges – in respect of such items as pilotage, lock operation and lighting – and consequently does not need to pass them on to port users, unlike most of the competing ports in other countries, at whose expense it has acquired a dominant role in Western Europe's seaborne trade.

Numerous instances of such *ad hoc* selective distortions of market forces can, of course, be found in every industrialized country and even in many LDCs. Many of them, naturally, are the result of political pres e from particular interest groups rather than part of a coherent industrial or economic strategy. They thus go to make up a confused pattern of what might be termed 'petty protectionism' – much of it often designed, in effect if not deliberately, to discriminate as much against different parts of the same country as against foreign competitors.

One example of this is the present British government's scheme of establishing Enterprise Zones, which are intended to stimulate economic activity in very small target areas of the country which are located at the heart of larger regions suffering from economic decay. This objective is supposed to be achieved by exempting establishments within each zone from local taxes and other burdensome regulations, although there is evidence that often the activity which is thereby induced is simply diverted from other parts of the United Kingdom – or even of the same city – where it would have occurred anyway. The growth and impact of such piecemeal measures, which have proliferated in the last 10 years of chronic recession, will be considered further in chapter 7.

Labour subsidies
One area of cost manipulation which is of central significance in considering how and why market forces have got distorted in the competitive struggle between both companies and countries is that of labour costs. For, as we have seen, the whole object of post-war macroeconomic policies in OECD countries has been (at least until very recently) to achieve and maintain full employment – and, by extension, a decent living standard for all citizens. The implication of this basic assumption is that the level of rewards to labour from paid employment – the most important determinant of living standards for most people – is not something which can be left to market forces alone to establish in the same way as is possible with the price of other factors of production such as capital, land and raw materials. Under these circumstances it is axiomatic that steps can legitimately be taken either to sustain wages above a minimum level by legislation or else to subsidize them by various means so that the social need to maintain wages and living standards does not conflict with the compulsion of private employers to maintain their competitiveness and pro-fitability.

The setting of statutory minimum wages is a practice common to most developed countries and many developing ones, although in Britain it has hitherto been largely eschewed. (This has been as much at the instance of the trade unions as of the employers – since the former have long been relatively powerful compared with their counterparts in other countries and have thus tended to see wage legislation, whether in relation to upper or lower limits, as weakening their bargaining role – and is confined to those industries where labour has traditionally been weakly organized). Wages as such in any case only comprise one component of labour costs, and most countries also have regulations governing such matters as social security and pension levels and contributions, sickness and holiday pay and compensation for redundancy. Needless to say, the levels at which standards are set in respect of these items, and the criteria used for doing so, vary widely between different countries. However, there is no doubt that, in all OECD countries at any rate, the post-war period witnessed a vast improvement in standards in these areas – along with a general upgrading of employment conditions (relating to health and safety at work, for example) which imposed further costs on employers.

Despite this increased burden on their finances, companies were for a long time not wholly antagonistic to these developments. Many were no doubt at least half convinced by the Keynesian argument that the maintenance of high and rising real income levels – distributed among the largest possible proportion of the population – was an important prerequisite of the rapid market expansion from which the corporate sector benefited during the 1950s and 1960s. At the same time many firms, particularly those operating mainly in distinct national markets (that is, non-multinationals), were not unhappy to see a limitation placed on the scope for inter-company competition in respect of such a large item as labour costs – a point recently confirmed by the noticeable lack of enthusiasm on the part of some employers for the Thatcher government's proposal to abolish the Wages Councils (the basis for the only form of minimum wage regulation in Britain). Similar considerations led many employers to support the introduction of officially enforced wage restraint – especially in times of relative labour scarcity – so as to reduce the danger of competitive bidding up of wages at the higher end of the scale.

Another way in which the burden of labour costs can be alleviated in cases where companies find it too onerous is by directly subsidizing them. At one extreme this can entail a state supplement to the wages of each employee in a given industry or area. An example of this in Britain was the Regional Employment Premium – in force from 1966 to 1973 – which was payable in respect of employees of establishments located in the more economically depressed areas of the country. A less direct, but at one time valued, form of assistance has been the subsidization of training programmes – something which companies have often been unwilling to pay for in full themselves in view of the danger that, in a tight and consequently competitive labour market, money spent by companies on training might too easily become a subsidy to competing firms willing and able to attract away their skilled workers with offers of improved terms. The cost of training has in fact been subsidized in most OECD countries at various times and in different degrees,[14] although latterly the programmes which were set up when skilled labour scarcity was a serious potential constraint on growth have tended to be replaced by ones whose purpose is the more cosmetic one of making a gesture in the direction of improving the job prospects of the increasingly large numbers of young unemployed.

Social infrastructure
Superficially it could be suggested that the net effect of all such government regulation is to place a tax rather than a subsidy on the use of labour. Indeed this was often the overall objective of government policy at times of relative labour scarcity – that is, before the onset of mass unemployment in the OECD economies from the mid-1970s. Yet the role of the modern state in subsidizing the private sector – particularly with regard to labour costs – is far more pervasive and subtle than is implied by such selective short-term subventions of wages and training outlays. For the entire apparatus of physical and social infrastructure – mostly financed out of public funds – constitutes an asset of which private companies can make profitable use, even though the community's investment in it is generally undertaken for much broader reasons than consideration of potential economic or commercial gains to the corporate sector, whether public or private.

Most obviously, the education system – which in the great majority of countries is at least 90 per cent state funded – provides (at least in OECD countries) a huge basic store of 'human capital' on which the private sector is free to draw and inevitably makes a far more effective (and costly) contribution to the competitiveness of industry than expenditure on more specific training of the type referred to above. Moreover, while it continues to be valued for its less tangible benefits as well – that is to say that in economic terms it is just as much a form of consumption as of investment – there is evidently a growing tendency on the part of politicians as well as economists to measure the performance of the education system in terms of its impact on the economy as a whole. (This is not least because of the perception that budgetary constraints in time of recession require a more rigorously selective use of resources.) This propensity was manifested in the 'great debate' about the future of education which the last Labour government sought to stimulate in Britain in the late 1970s, and in which the government itself strongly canvassed the view that the curriculum needed to be more closely geared to the needs of industry. This idea has subsequently borne fruit in a much greater emphasis on vocational training as an adjunct to or substitute for more academic secondary education. Whatever the merits of this approach – in either educational or economic terms – it has undoubtedly served to emphasize the extent to which such collective investment is a subsidy to those companies which make use of the assets it produces. Another well publicised instance of this tendency to see national education systems as a key element in the neo-mercantilist struggle for economic supremacy has been furnished by the recent expression of US worries about the failure of their system to produce graduates of as good quality as their Japanese counterparts in technology-related subjects.

Health services constitute another means by which the state helps to increase the quality and efficiency of the labour force, although compared with education its output must clearly be viewed much more as consumption than investment in so far as it is regarded as something desirable in itself irrespective of the economic benefits. Likewise it could be claimed that other social services provide an indirect benefit to the private sector to the extent that they facilitate the smooth functioning and expansion of commerce and industry or help to mitigate some of its adverse social consequences – for example, through provision of public housing or child care – while the value to private industry of efficient traditional services such as waste disposal is self-evident.

LDCs and the loaded dice

The logical extension of this argument might lead us to the conclusion that all forms of public service – even down to the police and the armed forces – are actually or potentially a form of subsidy to the private sector and thus preclude any genuinely undistorted competition. One does not, however, necessarily need to accept such remorseless logic in order to recognize that the enormous extension of the role of the welfare state in the OECD countries during the post-war era has also greatly increased the scope for distorting market forces in a mercantilist fashion,[15] if it has not wholly undermined the rationale of the market system. Seen from the perspective of national rather than corporate interests the significance of this development is that it has greatly increased the relative competitive strength of the industrialized countries compared with the LDCs. This is because the fiscal resources of the former in proportion to their population – not to mention their borrowing power in international markets – are so much greater than that of LDCs that, combined with their existing vastly superior endowment in infrastructure and technological expertise, it gives them a far greater capacity than the LDCs for using governmental power to distort market forces (already heavily biased in their favour) to extend their competitive advantage even further.

It is true that these advantages are partly offset by that of LDCs in respect of the cost of basic factors of production, especially that of labour, and that this has enabled such countries to obtain an increasing share of world markets for the less capital-intensive forms of manufacture – such as steel, shipbuilding and even motor vehicles. Yet rapidly changing technology – mainly developed and controlled by multinationals or governments based in developed countries – and the trend towards 'knowledge-intensive' forms of industry (for example, using robots instead of human labour) are bound to make any comparative advantage of LDCs based on cheap labour extremely precarious. Indeed any suggestion that the LDCs can exploit their 'asset' of cheap labour to develop their economies (as sometimes suggested by advocates of the 'appropriate technology' route to development in the Third World) ignores some uncomfortable realities. For it is apparent that even with a heavy emphasis on labour-intensive methods the supply of cheap labour in the world still so far exceeds the demand for it that it makes individual LDCs extremely vulnerable to competition from others. This tendency is well illustrated by the post-war history of the textile industry, which was a major source of growth and employment in Japan in the 1950s, but which has since progressively shifted its concentration from higher to lower labour cost countries in the Far East – a process which seems likely to continue, probably in the direction of Africa. By the same token, trading on the advantage of cheap labour in the absence of any other inevitably condemns the mass of their inhabitants to perpetual relative deprivation – thus negating what most people have supposed to be the whole objective of 'development'.

Furthermore, trade unionists (and non-multinational employers) could well argue that the cheap labour advantage enjoyed by LDCs is itself partly the result of distortions caused by government policy and is not simply the result of their 'naturally' high rates of unemployment. For the denial of trade union rights and of freedom of political expression, as well as the absence of what in the industrialized West would be regarded as minimum acceptable standards for terms and conditions of employment, are undoubtedly factors which can be and are turned to advantage by LDCs seeking to attract investment and boost their sales in export markets. Yet in order to avoid the possibility of unfair competition of this kind it would clearly be necessary not only for all countries participating in world trade to adhere to common standards regarding minimum rights and conditions for workers (not to mention standards relating to pollution control), but also to organize some international inspectorate to ensure enforcement. The difficulty of attaining such conformity, however, is underlined by the fact that not even any OECD countries have adopted all the ILO conventions relating to workers' rights and conditions – the only such international standards which exist – or are likely to do so in the foreseeable future. The primary purpose of these conventions is to prevent the exploitation of workers as an end in itself rather than to provide a basis for fair international competition. However, trade unions not surprizingly see the latter purpose as a logical extension of the former.

Yet if it is difficult to envisage all countries agreeing to adopt similar standards with regard to labour conditions (or most other factors affecting competitiveness), it is equally impossible to try and establish measurable trade-offs between the market distortions practised by different countries or groups of countries – for example, balancing the welfare state subsidies available in OECD countries against the absence of workers' rights in LDCs. For the essential and inescapable conclusion is not that some countries apply a greater degree of distortion than others, but that all countries do and must engage in it to some degree – and that the extent and manner of their doing so will ultimately depend on their perception of how far it is necessary or desirable and on the resources at their disposal.

NOTES

(1) Ironically the British government's conversion to the idea of loan subsidization – partly in response to claims that it has been an important factor in the superior industrial performance of West

Germany and Japan – has come at a time when many continental practitioners of this approach are having second thoughts, as their highly geared industries have found themselves financially very exposed to the prolonged downturn of recent years. See Finance For Industry, *The Capital Structure of Industry in Europe*. London 1981.

(2) The Federal Reserve Bank of Philadelphia, *Business Review* Jan./Feb. 1982.

(3) Mr Sam Armacost of the Bank of America, quoted in M. Mayer, *The Bankers*. London. W.H. Allen 1976.

(4) *Far Eastern Economic Review*, 9 August 1974.

(5) Among European OECD countries only West Germany, which has otherwise been rather less interventionist than other countries in the region, has had a budget of over $1 billion a year for R & D, though in relation to the size of its economy this is scarcely bigger than the UK figure.

(6) I.C. Magaziner and T.H. Hoult, *Japanese Industrial Policy*. London. Policy Studies Institute 1980.

(7) Herman Kahn, *The Emerging Japanese Superstate: Challenge and Response*. Hardmondsworth. Penguin 1973.

(8) That is, bringing together representatives of government, management and trade unions.

(9) At the same time the GATT has also from the beginning identified state procurement as one of the most pervasive non-tariff barriers to trade, although it has never been in a position effectively to control it (a situation which hardly seems to have been affected by the Agreement on Government Procurement – sponsored by the GATT – which entered into force in 1981).

(10) Costing over $300 billion in 1975 prices since the agency was established in 1961.

(11) An exchange between British Airways and Pan American Airways in January 1984 has cast interesting light on the different ways in which airlines receive subsidies in the interests of national aerospace industries. In reply to Pan Am's claim – which though obviously valid they could not permit themselves to concede – that their operations of the Concorde supersonic airliner were heavily subsidized by the British government, British Airways countered that Pan Am had received (among other forms of state assistance) direct operating subsidies for 20 years under the US Civil Aeronautics Act, amounting in total to 34 per cent of its present asset value.

(12) This justification has even become sufficiently respectable for companies to feel able to plead that failure to win orders from their own government will destroy their sales prospects in export markets.

(13) *International Business Week*, 20 February 1984.

(14) For example, in Britain via the Industry Training Boards and in the United States under the Comprehensive Employment and Training Act.

(15) Cf. G. Myrdal, *Beyond the Welfare State*, London. George Duckworth 1960.

CHAPTER 6

The Instruments of Intervention II: Distortion of Trade Flows

It would not perhaps be difficult to assemble a mass of circumstantial evidence sufficient to convince many that the rules of the GATT-based free trade system are so ineffective as to be almost irrelevant. Indeed the GATT's own reports are replete with instances of actual or alleged breaches of both the letter and the spirit of the Agreement – most of them relating to non-tariff barriers – which have been the cause of complaints to the Secretariat, although, as was suggested in chapter 2, such complaints probably represent only a fraction of the infringements which actually occur.

However, defenders of the GATT might reasonably argue that this does not prove that the rules themselves are defective but may simply demonstrate that there are insufficient means of enforcement. A more serious criticism must be based on the identification of systematic infraction or circumvention of the rules in ways which have been, in effect, officially condoned if not encouraged over a long period. It is not therefore the purpose of the present study to catalogue the myriad mechanisms devised in different countries – ranging from temporary reductions in the number of customs officials to changes in health regulations governing food products – to enable them to secure short- or long-term relief from their obligations under the GATT. Rather we are concerned to identify the ways in which the distortion of international market forces for protectionist purposes has been effectively institutionalized through the application of state power.

THE EXPORT PROMOTION MACHINE

As we have already noted, there has always been, even at the height of the post-war enthusiasm for 'open trade', an inescapable conviction that it was preferable for a country to be in surplus rather than deficit on its external account – even though either case is clearly a symptom of disequilibrium in terms of international trade theory. This perception obviously leads to a tendency to regard exports as more desirable than imports, and it is hardly surprizing to discover that, while governments have created numerous bodies to foster the growth of exports, in no country is there such an organization as an import promotion board or an imports credit guarantee department.

By contrast the machinery of state has increasingly been deployed in support of national export drives – often to decisive effect. Once again this is far from being a uniquely post-war phenomenon. However, the practice of giving systematic government support for exports has undoubtedly gone much further since World War II than in any previous epoch, and has been conspicuously extended and refined during the prolonged world recession of the decade since 1973. In this connection the pattern of British institutional support for exports may serve to illustrate what has been a universal tendency, even if – taken together with the other state-sanctioned forms of protectionism – it has clearly not been the most successful example.

The British government provides organized promotional support for UK exports through a number of institutions. Of these only the British Overseas Trade Board (BOTB) and the Export Credits Guarantee Department (ECGD) are exclusively dedicated to assisting exports. The role of the ECGD will be discussed later in this chapter in the context of the aid/credit subsidy nexus. The BOTB – established by the Heath administration in 1972 – provides a far broader range of support services, although these are designed primarily for the benefit of smaller companies for which the overhead costs associated with exporting are relatively great in relation to their resources. It provides help in the shape of basic market information, subsidization of detailed marketing research and financial support to approved trade missions and repesentation at overseas trade fairs. For small and medium firms breaking into a new foreign market for the first time it even offers loans of up to £150,000 at very low interest rates to cover half the cost of local overheads (such as setting up a local office or production of promotional material).

An essential complement to the BOTB – and one which, in terms of its cost to the taxpayer, is far more significant – is provided by British diplomatic missions abroad. In theory, of course, the primary role of these is that of 'diplomacy' – that is, political representation of the British government – and the furnishing of consular services. However, with the advent of modern telecommunications the former role of the diplomatic service has been rendered largely redundant and it has been thought necessary to find another justification for its existence – or rather for not drastically reducing its size and expense to the taxpayer. This, it was determined in the late 1960s,[1] was to be the task of promoting British commercial interests – a role which demonstrably needed to be fulfilled by someone, even though it was not necessarily obvious that the diplomatic service would be the most cost-effective agency for doing it. What is far more significant in the present context, however, is that it does not seem to have occurred to any of the advocates of this change to question the propriety – in terms of the spirit of the GATT – of thus extending the role of the state in subsidizing the sales efforts of British companies.

A similar lack of inhibition is noteworthy in connection with the increasing tendency, common to all industrialized countries, to bring the full weight of government authority to bear in support of bids by national companies for major export contracts. As well as opening up the possibility of financial subsidization in various guises (see later) this inevitably brings such deals into the arena of political relations between the countries involved. While the detailed substance of inter-governmental exchanges of this kind is seldom made public, it is clear that political favours are frequently given in return for commercial benefits. Perhaps the most obvious instance of this has been the attempted Arab boycott of Israel, compliance with which has undoubtedly been used as leverage to secure numerous contracts in Arab countries. Yet it would be naïve to suppose that similar political factors are not among the bargaining counters used by the numerous government missions –

frequently led by ministers – which now perambulate the globe in search of business for their increasingly beleaguered industries at home.

An illustration of the extent to which this practice is now entrenched in international commercial relations is the unabashed vigour with which the current British leadership has assumed the task of 'batting for Britain' despite its avowed commitment to abstain from government subsidization of the private sector. As Secretary of State for Trade and Industry, Mr Norman Tebbit is in charge of the government's programme of privatizing state-owned industries – being undertaken on the grounds that, in his own words, 'the government has no business to be involved in running them'. Yet he appears to see no contradiction between this policy and his own vigorous participation in the marketing efforts of British companies – in both the public and private sectors – by lobbying foreign governments on their behalf.

Export credit subsidies – aid as protectionism

In 1978 an official of the Pakistan National Shipping Company recounted how he had been ordered to embark on an overseas expedition to purchase six bulk carriers 'but not to pay for them' – and that he had fulfilled his instructions with no difficulty. This anecdote illustrates graphically the growing importance in recent years of subsidized credit in sustaining the level of world trade generally. In fact the rise in reliance on this mechanism can be traced back to its extensive use in connection with the disbursement of Marshall Aid in Europe in the late 1940s, when it was clearly thought justified as a subsidy to the then severely disadvantaged recipient countries.

There are two basic ways in which credit can be subsidized. The commonest and least obtrusive method is that of providing some form of guarantee to the lender that the loan will be repaid – a practice which, as we have seen, has been extremely common among developed countries in relation to investment projects at home. In the case of export contracts it is usually applied to long-term finance for projects in those countries with a chronic balance of payments problem – or a doubtful credit rating for some other reason. Where the borrower is a state agency or public corporation it is usual, particularly in LDCs, to seek a formal guarantee of repayment from the government or central bank of the recipient country. For a long time such guarantees were thought sufficient in most cases, as bankers convinced themselves that such 'sovereign borrowers' could never become technically insolvent and would thus always be able to assure repayment more or less on time. This belief – somewhat irrational in view of pre-war experience[2] – was what made possible so much improvident lending to LDCs in the early 1970s and the subsequent hopeless indebtedness of so many of the latter.

In addition, however, the government of the exporting enterprise may directly guarantee all or part of the loan – to the extent that, as has increasingly been the case since the mid-1970s, the guarantee of the borrower's government is seen as insufficient security – or may provide a credit insurance facility. The latter practice is the most common among the OECD countries, to which indeed it is largely confined[3] (partly perhaps because it is also necessarily a subsidy to the multinational banks, which are all OECD based). It also has a relatively ancient pedigree – notably in Britain, where the Export Credit Guarantee Department dates back to 1920. Such official credit insurance is notionally given on the basis of a strictly limited subsidy, in so far as premiums paid to the state agency responsible in each country are supposed – in conformity with OECD guidelines as well as with the spirit of the GATT – at least to cover the cost of claims. However, the agency would not normally expect to make a return on capital employed comparable with that of a private sector insurance company, which explains why such insurance – which tends to be for long-term finance covering large-scale capital projects – is not normally handled by the private sector. The non-commercial nature of the insurance in turn makes it possible to charge a lower rate of interest on such loans than would be demanded under normal market conditions – that is, without the risk premium which would, on the basis of proper actuarial calculations, be required to induce commercial banks to assume liability for default by the borrower.

The subsidy thus results from the government of the lender acting as, in effect, a non-profit making insurance company. It is against the internationally agreed rules for a government actually to write off any accumulated losses of public export credit agencies. However, given that they are none the less able to cover any operating deficits by borrowing[4] – so that in effect such losses can be subsumed under the national debt – there is in reality nothing to prevent them setting their premium rates at levels which are loss making in actuarial terms. At the same time market interest rates themselves can be artificially depressed by the application of various forms of exchange control – as is still the case in Japan, where the access of domestic savers to the international credit markets is severely restricted.

In addition to thus subsidizing loans through guarantees governments frequently offer a straight subsidy to the borrower's financial costs in cases where they they are particularly anxious to secure an export order. Such subsidies may either involve a lowering of the interest rate below market levels or else an exceptionally long maturity – possibly even with an initial 'grace period' of a few years in which no repayments of principal are required. If, as is frequently the case with credits of this kind, the borrower is an LDC, it is common to combine such concessional loans with an element of grant aid from the lender's government to constitute an overall 'financing package' designed to assure a decisive competitive edge *vis-à-vis* suppliers from other countries.

The extent to which 'aid' is often merely a disguised export subsidy in such a context is demonstrated by the frequency with which the aid budgets of OECD countries are used to finance projects which are not normally recipients of aid from the particular government concerned. Thus in 1983 the prospect of a $400 million contract to build an urban railway system for the city of Medellín in Colombia stimulated bids from various companies based in Britain, France, West Germany, Canada and others which included offers of aid in support of the project from the national governments of each bidder, though only in the event that their respective national consortia were awarded the contract. In no case were any of the European countries concerned regular donors of aid to Colombia – which indeed is far from being one of the poorest of LDCs.

It is because these financial arrangements are such a crucial part of any large capital project – and because of the intensifying international competition to be awarded such contracts – that our Pakistani shipping company buyer could contemplate touting his order for vessels worth hundreds of millions of dollars without any necessity to put up more than a minimal amount of hard cash. But while the shipbuilding industry may be an extreme case – with productive capacity having risen steadily since 1973 against the background of a stagnant or declining world market – one does not have to look far to find numerous other examples of how the international capital projects business has become a buyer's, or rather a borrower's, market. Thus Indonesia and Thailand have both in early 1984 succeeded in renegotiating contracts worth $200-300 million each which had already been awarded for major energy-related projects, with the sole purpose of securing more favourable financial arrangements. In both cases government ministers from each of the exporting countries concerned (Britain, France and Sweden) were closely involved in the negotiations, and indeed helped to secure final agreement by offering some icing on the cake in the shape of several million dollars' worth of grant aid.

It is perhaps in sub-Saharan Africa, however, that such subsidized financing packages have become most crucial in the competition for capital project contracts, largely because of the chronic structural weakness in the balance of payments position of virtually all the countries in the region, which has been heavily exacerbated in recent years by the combined impact of higher oil prices and lower prices for their export commodities. In fact it has reached the point where, as the representative of a major European electronics group told the author in the course of a visit to West Africa a few years ago, 'to have any chance of doing business here one must be able to supply not only the equipment but the money to pay for it as well.' Given the growing instability – political as well as economic – of most of Africa, such credit-based transactions can clearly only be undertaken if the company's home government is prepared to give (at least implicitly) some guarantee against default by the borrower.

The extent to which this approach to exporting has become generally entrenched – and the government's role as lender of last resort is increasingly vital – is perfectly illustrated by a call in 1983 from the London-based Brazilian Chamber of Commerce for the British government to contribute to a $2.5 billion IMF export credit package to Brazil on the grounds that its failure to do so would damage the prospects for British exports to Brazil. Bearing in mind that the latter's world-beating $80 billion foreign debt had already reduced it to such manifest insolvency that even the ECGD had suspended cover on new medium- or long-term credits, such a demand is a remarkable testament to the extent to which non-market considerations now outweigh traditional commercial factors in international trade.

Many of the practices just described are theoretically prohibited by international agreements or codes of practice – notably the OECD's so-called 'consensus' on export credits. However, it has proved difficult, if not impossible, to determine the basis of an equitable level of minimum interest rates and insurance premiums to be charged. The main reason for this has been the substantial variations in domestic market interest rates between different OECD countries, combined with the general instability of currency exchange rates which has prevailed in recent years. Officially guaranteed loans are normally denominated in the currency of the guarantor government, if only because to do otherwise would introduce a foreign exchange risk to add to that of default. Adherence to market-determined costs would therefore imply charging interest at rates prevailing within the lending country concerned. Yet since the level of interest rates within any given country is itself heavily influenced by government monetary and fiscal policy, there is in any event likely to be a degree of artificiality in it. The OECD consensus has achieved limited success in restricting the variation in rates applied by different member countries, but it is clearly faced with an impossible task in reaching a durably satisfactory solution, especially bearing in mind the lack of any agreed actuarial standards to be used in setting credit insurance premiums[5] and all the other distortions being applied, including the aid weapon.

The concept of development aid has in fact been systematically abused for the purposes of export subsidy ever since it became a significant factor in relations between the developed and developing worlds in the early 1960s. For where development finance – in the form of either subsidised loans or outright grants – is on a bilateral basis (in other words not channelled through multilateral agencies such as the World Bank) it is in the vast majority of cases 'tied' to purchases of goods or services in the donor country, even, in many instances, to the extent of excluding from the scope of aid any project costs incurred in the currency of the recipient country. However, for a long time it could at least be claimed that aid programmes were drawn up primarily on the basis of developmental considerations, whereas in recent years there has been an increasing tendency to see them largely as an adjunct to export promotion or, at worst, a means of crude political manipulation.

Food aid
Indeed nothing illustrates better the self-serving character of industrialized countries' aid policies than the United States' distribution of food 'aid' under the programmes of the US Agency for International Development (USAID) and of the Department of Agriculture (USDA) under Public Law 480.[6] For while ostensibly designed to avert sharp price increases for basic foodstuffs – if not famine – in LDCs, the practical effect of such subsidized exports is too often to depress prices unduly in national or regional markets, notably in Africa, thus discouraging local subsistence farmers from expanding their marketable surplus. At the same time they provide an outlet for US grain surpluses which would otherwise have the effect of depressing prices at home or in more commercial export markets – that is, in those countries which can afford to pay the market price. Whether or not, as is sometimes claimed, the principal purpose of such aid is to enable the US to manipulate world markets for foodstuffs in such a way as to extend and perpetuate its own dominance of them – for political as much as economic ends[7] – there is little doubt that it is informed more by the objective of advancing the interests of the US farm industry than by considerations of the development requirements of the LDCs. In this sense it should be seen as part of a government-backed marketing effort designed to assure for US farmers the highest possible share of world markets.

Thus for example, soyabean producers enjoy substantial support from the USDA both in monitoring world market developments in respect of edible oils and fats on a detailed country-by-country basis and, more particularly, in efforts to promote the demand for soyabeans in the more promising markets. In pursuit of the latter objective the American Soybean Association – with the administrative and financial support of the USDA – offers to train personnel of the oils and fats refining industries of selected LDCs (frequently in the United States itself, all expenses paid) in the extraction and refining of soyabean oil. Naturally this is designed to increase the trainees' familiarity with and preference for soya at the expense of competing oilseeds such as rape, sunflower or palm oil[8] – an objective which can also, of course, be furthered by judicious short-term use of PL 480 or other aid programmes to subsidize imports of the product from the US.

In one case known to the author this policy helped to give soya a dominant share of the oils and fats market in Morocco – a position enjoyed up to the early 1970s by rapeseed. This was achieved, moreover, as the result of a carefully coordinated attack on the regional market, centred on Spain, where the ASA had succeeded in establishing a sizeable outlet for soyabeans in the local crushing industry, which then exported crude oil to Morocco and other neighbouring countries for refining. This highly effective regional marketing strategy – actively supported as it was by the USDA – demonstrates that USA Inc. is just as much a reality as Japan Inc., even if its activities are confined to a relatively limited range of economic sectors.

That this is indeed regarded as wholly proper – and indeed that aid programmes are widely thought to be only justifiable to the extent that they do not conflict with American commercial interests, at least in the agricultural sphere – is attested by a concerted attempt on the part of the oilseed and dairy lobbies in 1976 to have US government influence brought to bear on the World Bank, with a view to blocking a cheap loan by the latter in support of expanded palm oil production in Indonesia. This demand was made quite unashamedly on the grounds that such a loan would be a subsidy to a major competitor with vegetable and animal fats produced in the US. This attitude is frankly summed up in the statement that 'neither we nor other rich countries are willing to forgo substantial foreign exchange earnings in the interests of feeding the poor.'[9] As this statement implies – and as it is only fair to point out – the US is not alone in seeking to solve the problems of its domestic farm industry at the expense of the rest of the world. Indeed the EEC – with its chronic tendency to produce enormous surpluses of grain, beef, dairy products, sugar and other commodities, which can only be disposed of by exporting them at a huge loss – has tended increasingly in recent years to rival the US as a source of world market disruption in the agricultural sector.

Political risk insurance
The United States has also pioneered a form of assistance to LDCs which constitiutes another thinly disguised form of protectionism, namely state insurance of private investment abroad in respect of

'political risk' – through the Overseas Private Investment Corporation (OPIC). This insurance – which covers US-owned companies
against loss through war, revolution, insurrection or expropriation
– is clearly designed to be more of a subsidy to US-based
multinational companies than to benefit the US trade balance.[10]
Yet in so far as such investments are likely to generate a demand
for goods and services from the US – through backward linkages
within the same group – as well as profits which can be remitted to
the US, this form of support is clearly an indirect form of
protectionism. It is a type of aid particularly favoured by the
Reagan administration, which prefers to see investment for
development undertaken by the private sector – albeit with the
assistace of public subsidies – rather than through government-to-
government loans or donations. Such collaboration between the
state and private industry in securing outlets in LDC markets is of
course practised, with varying degrees of subtlety and commitment, by several other OECD countries. France in particular has
achieved a remarkable symbiosis of the public and private sectors –
consistent with its long-standing corporatist traditions – in its
approach to winning and retaining export markets. The most
striking symptom of this relationship is the presence of the
government as a shareholder in many of the key French industrial,
trading, engineering and consultancy companies which constitute
the spearhead of the country's export effort, on top of which the
major banks have long been under full state control. This mutual
infiltration of public and private bodies can perhaps be observed at
its most blatant in former French colonies in sub-Saharan Africa,
where aid, trade and investment activities of various French
agencies and companies can often be found to be part of an
integrated strategy designed to advance French economic and
commercial interests – a policy made both more feasible and (from
the French standpoint) more necessary by the fact that most of the
countries concerned belong to the franc zone and are effectively
dependent on France for their supplies of hard currency.

Apart from its protectionist effect in favour of donor countries,
development aid also inevitably has a distorting impact on the
allocation of resources among and within LDCs. Indeed the entire
raison d'être of aid is the belief that market forces cannot on their
own be relied upon to produce politically acceptable results in all
circumstances. The danger is that, as aid programmes come to be

dominated more and more by non-developmental considerations, they inevitably tend only to replace one set of antisocial criteria for economic decision taking with another. This question, together with the manifest failure of more than two 'development decades' to bring a solution to the problem of Third World poverty any nearer, have begun to call in question as never before the validity of the whole concept of aid.

The manipulation of commodity markets

As noted earlier, the United States has not been averse to distorting world agricultural markets in the interests of supporting its farming community. Yet it has demonstrated also that it will not scruple to use its disproportionate financial and market power to manipulate food and other commodity markets in furtherance of what it sees as its national economic and political interests. Thus it operates a system of import quotas for sugar – with prices fixed at levels which are usually more remunerative than those prevailing on the open world market. These quotas are consequently much prized by the many LDCs which are dependent on sugar as a source of export earnings. Precisely for this reason the US government is able to use the offer of such quotas (or the threat to withdraw them) as a means of political leverage, although this fact normally only comes to public attention when such threats are carried out – as when in 1983 Nicaragua was deprived of its quota by the Reagan administration, which sought to weaken the leftist Sandinista regime.

In addition the US government has long maintained stockpiles of key commodities such as copper, tin and rubber, on the grounds of the need to hold strategic reserves against the possibility of a disruption in supply for whatever reason. Yet the existence of these stockpiles – the level of which can naturally be varied at any time – has also given the United States a means, which it has shown itself quite willing to use, to influence the level of prices on world markets.

The fact that these weapons are seen as useful from the standpoint of exclusively American interests is underlined by the tendency of the US to hold aloof from efforts to establish international agreements for the stabilization of commodity markets, many of which have come to grief precisely for this reason. For the essence of such agreements is a concerted attempt to stabilize prices by means of agreed export and import quotas for the main exporting and importing countries, usually with the additional back-up of a buffer stock which can in theory be used – in the same way as the US stockpiles – to even out any otherwise uncontrollable disruption of the market. It may be remarked in passing that, despite their extremely limited success, such agreements have arguably provided a precedent for the increasing tendency – which will be discussed in later chapters – to try and cartelize markets for manufactured goods as well, although this has not yet been attempted on anything approaching a global basis.

Exchange rate manipulation
For over 25 years one of the pillars of the International Monetary Fund, and indeed of the whole Bretton Woods system was the regime of fixed exchange rates centred on the US dollar as the major reserve currency. In the eyes of Keynes and the other founding fathers of the system the importance of maintaining stability in the parities of major currencies was one of the central lessons of the international monetary chaos of the pre-war period, when unilateral currency devaluation was frequently used as a protectionist weapon by many countries, often with a devastating effect on the level of trade.

We have already briefly charted the course of events which led to the demise of this regime in 1971 and identified the main cause of this as the irreconcilable differences between national economic policies – compounded by political friction. The surprisingly positive reaction which initially greeted this breakdown in the post-war order has also been noted. The fact that few appeared to see in it either a potential source of monetary instability or a threat to the 'open' trading system is perhaps a measure of the euphoria which still gripped even the most informed opinion after a generation of seemingly limitless expansion in the Western World. The period of pre-war 'beggar-my-neighbour' policies was by then a distant memory and perhaps few could imagine a return to systematic protectionism after a period in which the growth of world trade and national living standards had marched so harmoniously together. Equally, in an era when the demand for 'deregulation' was an increasingly fashionable cry – particularly in all matters financial – it was easy to portray the preference for fixed parities as the outmoded shibboleth of a bygone era.

What is at first sight more difficult to understand is why the subsequent collapse of the post-war boom – precipitating the persistent low growth of the decade since 1974 – has not led to any searching reappraisal of the initial enthusiasm for abandoning fixed exchange rates. It is true that the absurdity of the proposition – widely cherished in the early 1970s – that a regime of 'floating' rates would absolve governments from the restricting need to defend particular parities for their currencies, and thus liberate expansionist forces, is now tacitly recognized. Indeed it has become obvious that a freely fluctuating currency exposes an economy to intolerable instability and that governments must therefore have both a view as to the appropriate value of their currency in terms of others and policy instruments designed to keep it close to whatever target level is deemed appropriate.

Yet there is still no significant body of opinion which supports an attempt to restore an internationally agreed structure of fixed parities. The only apparent exception to this continuing predilection for free exchange rate movements is the attempt by the EEC since 1978 to establish a measure of intra-community currency stability through the European Monetary System (EMS), whereby eight of the ten currencies of member states (sterling and the Greek drachma are at present excluded) are committed to prevent their exchange rates from fluctuating outside a narrow range against the European Currency Unit, whose value *vis-à-vis* third country currencies is itself based on a 'basket' of community currencies. Yet the purpose of this arrangement – which in any case remains extremely tenuous – is primarily to facilitate the functioning of the Common Market itself, which by the mid-1970s was increasingly threatened with total breakdown as a result of the impact of currency fluctuations on the administration of the Common Agricultural Policy.

Once it became generally accepted that the value of a country's currency can never be a matter of indifference to its government, the word 'floating' was rendered largely meaningless as a description of the international exchange rate system. Likewise the term 'dirty floating', sometimes used to denote the distorted fluctuations of currency values resulting from uncoordinated interventions by governments to influence the international value of their currencies, is misleading in so far as it implies an aberration from a system in which currency values are basically determined by the free play of market forces. For, as was suggested in chapter 3, the conventional pursuit of macroeconomic policy objectives by means of fiscal and monetary manipulation is bound to influence, as well as be influenced by, the external position of a national economy and thus the market value of its currency.

It is therefore a contradiction in terms to suggest that any country can or should allow its currency's value to fluctuate freely – except in the case of those LDCs whose fiscal and foreign exchange resources are so meagre that they are unable in any event to pursue an independent macroeconomic policy in the sense in which OECD countries do. To that extent the ending of the fixed exchange rate commitment has imposed an added disadvantage on the countries of the Third World, which are so weak that they have to accept the imposition from outside of the value of their currencies – often having to endure lectures from the IMF on the virtues of giving market forces their head – while those countries which effectively run the IMF and control the international financial system (that is, the OECD group) are to a considerable extent free to manipulate the impact of market forces on their currencies and thereby give them an artificial value.

This is particularly easy where the objective is to depress the currency's value with a view to both gaining a competitive advantage in export markets and protecting the domestic market. Without necessarily proclaiming a formal devaluation the government (usually through the central bank) can manipulate the currency's value both by its operations in the foreign exchange markets and by means of variations in official interest rates. In addition exchange controls – which are normally applied in such a way as to keep a currency's value artificially above what would otherwise be the market rate – can also be used to the opposite effect. Thus Japan has been able, by simultaneously enforcing low domestic interest rates and barring most of its citizens from access to overseas financial markets, both to discourage the inflow of foreign funds and to prevent an outflow of domestic funds in search of the higher interest rates which are available elsewhere. It has thus been able largely to insulate the Japanese economy from the destabilizing effects of 'hot' money flows which affect other OECD economies and – as demonstrated since 1981 – to prevent the yen exchange rate from rising at a time when the economy's relative competitiveness, as reflected in its burgeoning balance of payments surplus, has been remorselessly increasing.[11]

Those who maintain a fairly complacent view of this unstructured pattern of exchange rates can perhaps argue that there is still sufficient recognition on the part of governments and central banks of the need to prevent sudden massive disruptions of the currency markets to ensure that adjustments are relatively orderly. Indeed it is true that sharp competitive devaluations – such as that carried out in Sweden by the incoming Social Democratic government in 1982 – are relatively rare and confined to smaller countries. However, the important point is that governments are – with the partial exception of the members of the EMS – no longer tied by the discipline of maintaining a fixed parity and can consequently pursue policies which lead to a gradual depreciation of their currencies without infringing any rules but at the same time artificially undercutting their foreign competitors. Admittedly a policy of currency depreciation is no guarantee of improving an economy's relative competitiveness, since it may precipitate a boost to domestic inflation which will tend to erode the initial price advantage. In many cases governments have sought to circumvent this danger by resorting to another form of intervention which amounts to suppressing the symptoms of inflation – namely prices and incomes policies.

PRICE AND WAGE CONTROLS

Among the various forms of market distortion employed by governments to give their economies an advantage over foreign competitors, price and wage controls are a somewhat distinctive phenomenon. This is because, whereas most other forms of intervention with this end in view take the form of a state subsidy to one kind of economic activity or another, price and wage controls – at least as applied to the private sector – amount to a forced subsidy by companies and/or wage earners to the benefit of the national economy, and in particular to its international competitiveness. It was a technique of market distortion which had a considerable vogue in Western Europe in the 1960s and 1970s, when support for it was chiefly identified with those Keynesian economists who preached that the inflationary consequences of what they saw as excess demand – particularly for labour – could be averted by means of the administratively enforced restriction of increases in the costs of factors of production (including wages) and in output prices. It thus held out, according to its proponents, the possibility of combining rapid economic growth with relatively stable prices and the maintenance, if not improvement, of national economic competitiveness.

To enter here into the arguments for and against wage and price restraint would be an undue digression. The significance of such measures in relation to the present argument has to do not with their effectiveness – which was often real over the very short term, though less obviously so in the longer term – but with the fact that they have become acceptable practice in terms of the rules of the international market economy game; this despite the fact that they clearly amount to official interference with the normal processes of price and income determination. (In this connection it is worth recalling that even a government so steeped in economic ortho-doxy as the Nixon administration in the US made a thoroughgoing – albeit short-lived – attempt to institutionalise such controls). Indeed the long-term importance of the recognition of price and income controls as valid instruments of economic policy is precisely its implication that such 'normal processes' may tend to produce results which a politically unacceptable. At one level this argument rests on the belief that prices and wages are in any case no longer (if they ever were) determined by market forces (except perhaps in the very long run) but rather by agreement between unholy combinations of big business and trade unions – that is, the corporatist 'technostructure' of Professor Galbraith, himself a fervent and long-standing advocate of official price and wage controls.[12] But in the eyes of the governments which have practised such controls the case for them does not depend on whether or to what extent the market has ceased to be competitive. For from the standpoint of the public interest even genuinely untrammelled competition – if such could ever be realized – might still result in a level of relative decline in national output which would be inconsistent with established social or political objec-tives.

Yet if the resort to managed wage and price levels implied scepticism as to the ability of the market to produce a satisfactory distribution of income or allocation of resources, it also necessarily introduced non-market criteria into the equation. In essence these all turned on judgments concerning equity or fairness – that is, as to the levels of profit deemed appropriate to assure an acceptable rate of return to the shareholders in a particular industry and the levels of wages comparable with those available in similar industries or occupations. The task of the authorities responsible for the administration of price and wage controls (such as the now defunct National Board for Prices and Incomes in Britain) was to reconcile these criteria with those of efficiency and the need to be competitive in international markets. Thus in a sense the idea of such centralized control over costs and prices comes close to a resurrection of the medieval concept of the 'just price' – most closely associated with St.Thomas Aquinas and the Schoolmen – which is usually regarded as the very antithesis of *laissez-faire* ideology.[13] Yet while the application of such criteria can to a limited extent be realized within the boundaries of an individual country, there is clearly at present no basis for common international standards to be established or, if there were, to be enforced – although, as will be shown in chapter 8, acceptance of the principle is implicit in the fixing of minimum import prices for steel in the US and the EEC.

Enough evidence has perhaps been adduced in the last two chapters to demonstrate beyond reasonable doubt that the supposed commitment of the post-war Western World to the ideal of free trade was no more genuine than that of previous generations, and that the only distinctive feature of the period since 1945 was that the availability of a vast new armoury of protectionist weapons permitted countries to dismantle traditional tariff barriers with scarcely a qualm. If this conclusion is valid it should serve to correct the popular belief that the widely observed growth in protectionist pressures and measures since the mid-1970s is uniquely the product of the prolonged recession which dates from that time. Nevertheless it is undeniable – as suggested by several of the examples already cited – that the recession has greatly exacerbated the tensions and contradictions of a world economic and commercial order which had already been severely weakened by the collapse of the Bretton Woods system in 1971. The scale and consequences of this progressive lapse into anarchy we now turn to consider.

NOTES

(1) Report to the Committee on Overseas Representation (the Duncan Report). HMSO 1968.

(2) A large amount of sovereign debt, notably that of Germany, proved ultimately worthless after the European financial debacle of 1931.

(3) Although recent suggestions that the World Bank may provide an export credit facility for Brazil – a measure of that country's desperate balance of payments plight – indicate that this may not be the case for much longer.

(4) In recent years the export credit agencies of Britain, Japan, Italy, Sweden, Switzerland and France have all begun to record annual deficits, whereas previously they mostly produce operating surpluses.

(5) These currently range from 0.2 per cent to 6 per cent of insured value, depending on the precise nature of the cover as well as on the government providing it, with those charged by the Export Insurance Department of Japan being much the cheapest.

(6) Otherwise known as the Food for Peace Law, this dates from 1954. It should be noted that the food is not normally donated as such but sold for local currency, thus making the US government an effective creditor of the country concerned to the value of the food supplied.

(7) Considerable credence was lent to this theory by President Ford's Secretary for Agriculture, Mr Earl Butz, who openly asserted that food was a major weapon in the American diplomatic arsenal.

(8) Such use of 'technical assistance' – potentially perhaps the most cost-effective form of development aid – as an export marketing device is increasingly popular among all OECD countries in their effort to secure outlets for manufactured goods as well as agricultural products.

(9) Lyle P. Schertz (Deputy Administrator, Economic Research Service, US Department of Agriculture) in *Foreign Affairs*, April 1974. Quoted in S. George, *Les Stratégies de la Faim*. Geneva. Editions Grouaneur 1980.

(10) In Britain the ECGD has recently taken a tentative step down the same road with the announcement of its intention to offer cover against war risk in cases where private sector insurance companies cannot or will not provide it.

(11) It has also permitted the Japanese government to pursue and extremely lax fiscal policy, covering its persistently huge budget deficits by massive borrowing at low rates of interest (so that it now has a proportionately much greater national debt burden than any other major OECD country).

(12) J.K. Galbraith, *The New Industrial State*. London. Hamish Hamilton 1967.

(13) Cf. R.H. Tawney, *Religion and the Rise of Capitalism*. Harmondsworth. Penguin 1961.

CHAPTER 7

The Impact of Recession

It is generally agreed that 1973 is to be considered a watershed year in the post-war history of the world economy. This is because it was the last year of a boom which had lasted since the late 1940s, bringing with it unprecedentedly sustained growth throughout the Western World. There had of course been partial downturns in activity during this period – notably in the late 1950s in the United States – but these were never so severe or so general as to constitute a major interruption to the momentum of growth, or (which was the crucial factor) to damage confidence that growth would be sustained.

ORIGINS OF THE POST-1973 DOWNTURN

It was precisely the breakdown in this confidence which distinguished the events of 1973 – affecting every country in the OECD and many LDCs as well – and precipitated a recession of a severity not seen since the 1930s. However, as with so many turning points in history – economical or political – the disjunction was far less sudden and more complex in its origins than is implied by the ascription to it of a particular date or event. In this respect the quadrupling of posted prices by the Organization of Petroleum Exporting Countries (OPEC) in the last quarter of 1973 – for long popularly supposed to have been the principal, if not the sole, cause of the West's subsequent economic ills – may be seen to have been a scarcely more decisive event than the assassination of Archduke Franz Ferdinand at Sarajevo in June 1914, the incident usually held to have sparked off World War I. The convenience of

OPEC as a scapegoat was all the greater because its membership consisted entirely of LDCs – a fact which made it possible for politicians and the mass media to portray its actions as some kind of anti-Western plot. The reality is that the upsurge in OECD output which immediately preceded the OPEC oil shock (in 1972-73) was of a febrile character and largely based on speculative impulses – of which the mounting inflationary pressures were arguably both cause and effect – and that this in turn reflected widespread loss of confidence in the scope for continuing expansion based on apparent market prospects. Against this background, in which inflation had already reached alarming levels by mid-1973, the OPEC action – drastic though it was – may be seen as more of a response to than a cause of the worldwide economic upheaval.

Admittedly the underlying causes of the subsequent recession – which can be said to have continued to the present day despite periodic but short-lived 'recoveries' – are more complex than a simple slackening of demand growth, as we shall have occasion to show in the course of this chapter. Yet in the present context the most significant fact regarding the post-1973 debacle – and the most uncomfortable one for would-be defenders of the 'open' trading system – is that, wherever the blame for it might lie, it can scarcely be laid at the door of protectionist tendencies. It is true, as has been shown in earlier chapters, that a wide range of *de facto* protectionist measures and practices were being applied before 1973. Yet it has also been the author's contention that it was the widespread legitimization of state intervention in national economies which made such neo-protectionism possible and the lowering of conventional tariff barriers acceptable. If as against this one rejects the significance of this form of protectionism and is content to equate trade liberalization with tariff reduction, and if one also upholds the belief that liberalization is a precondition for the expansion of trade (and prosperity in general) then one has to explain why the recession took hold in the middle of the protracted series of tariff cuts which occurred at regular intervals under the GATT from the time of its inception (negotiations on the latest so-called Tokyo Round began in 1974).

THE PROTECTIONIST RESPONSE – CARTELIZATION

But if there is a lack of empirical evidence to support the view that free trade begets prosperity[1] and protectionism the converse, there can be little dispute that recession increases the tendency to resort to protectionism – however great or slight it may have been to begin with. Yet precisely because the scope for covert protectionism was so immense throughout the post-war period – while the slide into recession was gradual, and not at first generally recognized to be a long-term phenomenon – there was no sharp break with previous commitments to trading partners, as occurred for example after the Great Crash of 1929, when the US Hawley/Smoot Act marked a clear and deliberate retreat from open trade, to be followed by similar measures in Europe and elsewhere.

In fact one development which has perhaps come to be regarded as most typical of the pattern of recession-induced protectionism since 1973 – the Multi-Fibre Agreement (MFA) governing textile exports from LDCs to developed countries – was largely formulated in the years before 1973,[2] though not formally inaugurated until 1974 after protracted negotiations. This agreement, sponsored and monitored by GATT, amounted to an officially sanctioned cartelization of most of the world market for textiles and clothing. As such it was a response to the rapidly increasing penetration of OECD textile markets by LDC suppliers, notably those in the Far East. Since this threatened to enforce the rapid rundown of large parts of the industry in OECD countries, political pressures – exerted both by the companies under threat and by organized labour – required that something should be done to limit the danger. At the same time it was clear that action under Article XIX of the GATT, permitting temporary protective action in support of a particular threatened industry, would not suffice in this case, given the fundamental competitive advantage enjoyed by the LDCs in respect of most textile products (derived from the relatively high labour intensity of the industry and their low labour costs). Equally, resort to subsidies or other non-tariff forms of protection would be both costly to OECD taxpayers and politically undesirable in the context of the developed nations' avowed commitment to assist the LDCs to improve their economic situation by (among other things) diversifying and expanding their exports to developed countries.

The MFA constituted an attempt at compromise between these sharply conflicting constraints. The idea was to ensure a controlled expansion of LDC textile exports (originally intended to be at the rate of 6 per cent a year), designed to spread the burden evenly among the importing industrialized countries and to ensure that individual LDCs also obtained a fair share of the expanding market. This was achieved through a series of bilateral agreements between individual exporting and importing countries under the global GATT umbrella. This arrangement, which has always been regarded as profoundly unsatisfactory by the LDCs, was effectively imposed on them at pistol point, in that the industrialized countries indicated that the alternative was more thoroughgoing protectionist measures. In operation it has proved even less satisfactory, largely because the recession – which was clearly not anticipated when the original agreement was signed – has cut the growth of demand in OECD countries below what was then forecast. This has been reflected in the subsequent agreements governing the renewal of the MFA – in 1977 and 1981 – which widened the latitude permitted to the importing countries for suspending their commitments to LDC textile exporters.

A significant aspect of the MFA is that it was an early symptom of one of the crucial factors in the post-1973 recession – the growth of global productive capacity, particularly in the LDCs. Indeed the fact that it was negotiated before the recession became a reality reflects the fact that the danger of oversupplied world markets – as much as an actual fall-off in the growth of demand – was an important cause of the declining growth of productive investment which was noticeable among OECD countries from the late 1960s (the annual average growth of gross fixed capital formation in the OECD fell from 6.7 per cent in the 1960-65 period to 4.6 per cent in 1970-73, before turning negative in 1973-78).

Yet the greatest importance of the MFA perhaps lies in the fact that it provided a precedent – if not exactly a model – for the cartelization of other world markets. In fact other cartels have to date been far less comprehensive or formal,[3] but the principle of cartelization – that is, allocating specific market shares of national or regional markets to suppliers of particular nationalities – has become increasingly well established. This is particularly true of trade between OECD countries, where such arrangements often take the form of 'voluntary restraint' agreements, such as those affecting Japanese exports of motor vehicles, TV sets and video recorders to the EEC and the United States. Such understandings do not in theory amount to a guaranteed minimum share of the market, as they only place a ceiling on the amount of the item concerned which can be imported within a given period. In practice, however, the maximum naturally tends to become the minimum, especially where there is negligible overall growth in the market and domestic producers therefore have less incentive to invest in new and more efficient plant. Moreover, in the case of such Japanese exports the exporters themselves – or those who are fortunate enough to obtain a sizeable share of the quota – are often only too happy to acquiesce in the arrangement, since it sharply reduces their need to compete on price and thus makes their total level of exports to the market concerned both more predictable and more profitable.

This trend towards cartelization based on government-backed agreements has its counterpart in less formal, purely private sector, arrangements. Yet it should scarcely need to be pointed out that such cooperation between companies across frontiers – often facilitated, where this is thought necessary, by a formal relaxation of anti-monopoly restrictions – amounts to cartelization just as much as where governments are formally involved in regulating it.

This practice has naturally affected those mature industries where market growth has levelled off while competition (especially from LDC suppliers) has increased. Collaboration between motor manufacturers – most notably in the shape of design and technology sharing and reciprocal marketing arrangements – has been increasingly conspicuous. This kind of link was originally pioneered by General Motors and the other major US motor corporations in deals with their Japanese counterparts in the 1960s, though at that time the purpose was primarily to circumvent restrictions on foreign investment in Japan. Recently, however, the object of most such joint ventures has been rather to get round limitations, actual or potential, on Japanese exports to other OECD markets. Most spectacularly, General Motors, which had already been importing cars made by Isuzu Motors (in which it has long had a large minority shareholding) to complement its model range in the US market, has in 1984 teamed up with two other

Japanese car makers – Suzuki, in which it has also taken a small shareholding, and Toyota, the largest Japanese producer of all. The arrangement with Suzuki is similar to that with Isuzu, though involving other markets besides the US, while the deal with Toyota will involve producing one of the latter's models in one of GM's own otherwise redundant factories. Yet another component of GM's strategy to neutralize competition from the Far East is a joint venture in South Korea with that country's second largest motor manufacturer, Daewoo.

The fact that the Federal Trade Commission has approved a combination between the world's two largest car manufacturers – not to mention the marketing deals with Isuzu and Suzuki – is a remarkable measure of the extent to which anti-trust principles are at a discount in the face of recession and the desperate struggle for markets. Similar pressures in the European market have led to production and marketing links between Honda and British Leyland and between Nissan and both Alfa Romeo and Volkswagen. Once again these deals have emphasized both the growing dominance of the Japanese vehicle industry – along with the mounting obstacles to its further penetration of European markets – and the inability of its smaller and weaker competitors to stay in the race while relying purely on their own resources.[4]

THE NEW TECHNOLOGY AND NATIONAL COMPETITIVENESS

Yet the most striking feature of this recent trend towards collaboration and concentration of forces among multinationals in the face of market uncertainty is that it has been most marked not in those mature industries where demand is relatively static but in the very 'sunrise' sector – electronics – that is virtually the only area of manufacturing certain to experience significant growth in the foreseeable future. Thus, for instance, an agreement was reached in 1983 between the US telecommunications giant American Telephone and Telegraph (AT&T) and Olivetti – the largest European-owned manufacturer of computers and typewriters – whereby each company would market the products of the other in their own respective home markets, while at the same time sharing technology and collaborating in the development of new products. At the same time AT&T – which had concluded a similar, though less far-reaching, deal with the Dutch giant Philips earlier in the same year – was to take a 25 per cent shareholding in Olivetti, with an option to raise this to 40 per cent after four years. (Ironically this move by AT&T towards restricting competition on an international basis followed immediately upon – and indeed was largely the consequence of – an anti-trust suit in the United States which resulted in the enforced divestiture by the company of most of its telecommunications business there.)

In the same way the French telecommunications equipment industry – fully state owned and rationalized under a single company (CIT-Alcatel) since 1982 – has sought cooperation agreements with its counterparts in West Germany and Britain, including a proposal that the telecommunications markets of France and the United Kingdom should be effectively cartelized between itself and the British firms Plessey and GEC. Likewise agreement was reached early in 1984 between the US and Japanese governments to facilitate joint research and development projects between US telecommunications companies and the Japanese state-owned telephone company, Nippon Telegraph and Telephone (NTT), with the ultimate object of boosting US sales of equipment to NTT. At the same time Fujitsu – Japan's largest computer company has taken (also at the beginning of 1984) a 49 per cent stake in Amdahl, one of the fastest growing smaller computer companies in the US, and also has joint marketing arrangements with Siemens and ICL, the major locally owned computer manufacturers in West Germany and Britain respectively. Within the EEC such inter-company cooperation across frontiers is now seen as the key to efforts to close the gap in competitiveness between the Community's electronics industry and those of Japan and the United States. To facilitate and encourage the process it has initiated a Community-wide R & D programme – the European Strategic Programme for Research and Development in Information Technology (ESPRIT) – which seeks to overcome the fragmentation of the industry in Europe and avoid duplication in a joint effort to bridge the gap with its rivals in the US and Japan, while it also offers large financial subsidies to companies engaged in joint developments. Moreover, in order to remove any possible inhibitions to such oligopolistic behaviour the EEC Commission has announced a draft amendment to Article 85 of the Treaty of Rome – which in theory precludes such anti-

competitive agreements between companies in the Community –
which would instead permit them in cases where they would
'contribute to the improvement of the production or distribution of
goods or to the promotion of technical or economic progress'.

In doing this, it should be emphasized, it is merely catching up
with long-standing practice in Japan – where the concept of
anti-trust regulation has never been the subject of more than polite
lip-service. Likewise, as already noted in respect of its motor
industry, the United States has shown few qualms in jettisoning its
commitment – traditionally much stronger than in any other
OECD country – to the maintenance of competition, as further
demonstrated by the government's sympathetic view of increasing
concentration in the oil and steel industries. In thus bowing to
political pressure from the business community, President Reagan
has made it clear that, unlike some members of the Thatcher
government in Britain, he is in no danger of letting free market
ideology get in the way of support for big business.

The fact that both governments and companies are increasingly
unwilling to leave it to the marketplace to determine the allocation
of resources in the electronics and allied industries reflects a
number of influences which are only partly associated with the
recession as such. Above all electronics, with its rapidly advancing
technology, is seen as the key to success in what is widely billed as
the 'second industrial revolution', with its multiplicity of applications (actual or potential) in virtually every branch of both
production and service sectors. It is therefore increasingly perceived that a country's prospects of ultimate prosperity depend on
its having independent access to and control of this technology and
also that it is impossible to achieve this by relying on market forces
alone. Governments thus tend to conclude that they must take the
initiative in promoting and financing the development of an
adequate national capability in this field, while the private sector is
equally aware that it needs public money to underwrite its
investment in such high technology developments – which also
entail high risks.

It is thus apparent that the necessity for countries to intervene in
the electronics sector is by way of being a self-fulfilling prophecy.
For it has already been observed in earlier chapters how the United
States has expended vast fiscal resources – both through military
programmes, the space programme and its official funding of

civilian research and development in various institutions – to assure for itself a lead in this and other branches of technology. Given this advantage, as well as the benefit of its vast domestic market in achieving economies of scale in production and distribution, it is scarcely surprising that other Western countries should have felt compelled to follow a similarly interventionist strategy in order to remain competitive.

Inevitably, therefore, as more and more countries have sought to enter the field of high technology industry with the aid of state subsidies under one guise or another, it has become increasingly impossible for any country to contemplate doing so without such subsidies, given the cost advantages which would otherwise be enjoyed by its competitors. This point has of course been most readily appreciated by private sector electronics companies. For, while anxious to be among the leaders in the development of new technology, they have been unable to afford to commit substantial amounts of their own money to the attainment of this objective in the knowledge that a large proportion of their competitors' costs has been effectively assumed by the state and that there is therefore little chance, other things being equal, of a purely commercial operation being able both to compete on price and to achieve an acceptable rate of return on capital.

Two other factors militate against the spontaneous, unaided involvement by the private sector in the development of the new technology generally – that is, covering such areas as biotechnology as well as microelectronics. These are the great uncertainty which still surrounds the commercial application of many of the new products it is generating, and the very speed of technological change, which brings with it the danger of early obsolescence and uncompetitiveness of newly installed productive capacity. Such dangers are all too clearly underlined by the sudden profits collapse experienced by a number of computer companies in 1983 – for example, Atari, Osborne – whose initial bubble of commercial success burst under the impact of fickle consumer interest and the arrival of new and cheaper products.

Taken together these developments prompt the rather bizarre conclusion that the new technology industries have assumed many of the economic characteristics of agriculture, in so far as they are officially viewed as industries which need to be supported at a minimum level of activity for 'strategic' reasons regardless of commercial viability. In the same way the development of such technology – which in many cases is indeed undertaken for strategic reasons in the narrowest (that is, military) sense of the term – has spawned a whole range of products for which the demand is uncertain and which, if it exists at all, may well be below what the advocates of such 'spin-off' benefits of military-based research programmes often seek to suggest. While we are clearly a long way from seeing the rise of 'mountains' of computer hardware or software – comparable to those of butter or beef which are accumulated under the agricultural policies of both the US and the EEC – it is equally clear that market forces are far from being the only, or indeed the predominant, influence determining the pattern of production in these industries.[5]

THE UNEMPLOYMENT CATASTROPHE

Yet if strategic factors, however broadly defined, have been increasingly important in sustaining the compulsion of governments to subsidize particular industries, they have been as nothing in significance compared with the political pressure to retain and create jobs in face of the mounting toll of unemployment. The decade from 1973 to 1983 witnessed a rise in the numbers of recorded unemployed in the OECD countries from just under 10 million to over 32 million (or from just over 3 per cent to around 9 per cent of the labour force). As was recalled in earlier chapters, the central preoccupation of economic policy makers in the aftermath of World War II – and one which inspired the design of the Bretton Woods system to a great extent – was the need to minimize, if not actually eliminate, unemployment. Although by the early 1960s the danger of mass unemployment appeared to have been banished – for ever, as many supposed – the fear of it was still sufficiently potent to make politicians feel that virtually any measures could be justified to avert its recurrence. While these attitudes have perforce been transformed by the events of the 1970s and 1980s, and OECD countries have to some extent learned to live with the reality of high numbers of jobless, it remains true that the commitment to fight unemployment is stronger among most governments than their commitment to the rules of the GATT.

Employment considerations are of course part and parcel of the ultimate justification for subsidizing high technology developments. Yet it is increasingly apparent that the impact of the new technology is mainly negative in relation to the level of employment in both manufacturing and services – as a result of the enormous gains in productivity which it usually brings with it. This has raised the spectre of unemployment continuing at high levels even in the event of a sustained revival of economic growth – a possibility which economists had previously largely discounted.[6] This has consequently intensified the pressure in OECD countries to protect those traditional domestic industries – such as steel, shipbuilding, motor vehicles, and textiles – which are still relatively labour intensive but which are faced with stagnant demand and increasing world-wide competition.

However, it is also hard to ignore the fact that these established manufacturing industries are the main basis of the industrialization plans of many LDCs – a tendency which, as we have seen to apply to textiles in the context of the MFA, it is difficult to resist totally, given the avowed support of OECD countries for the development of the LDCs. The claim of the latter to a greater share of world manufacturing output was enshrined in the so-called Lima declaration of 1975 – sponsored by the United Nations Industrial Development Organization (UNIDO) – which set a target of raising this share from 7 per cent to 25 per cent by the end of the century. While this precise goal has never been endorsed by most OECD countries – and indeed most of the other demands of the so-called Group of 77 LDCs in connection with their call for a 'new international economic order' have been rejected outright by the developed countries – the pressures on the latter were strong enough to make them shrink from any overt discrimination against the manufactured exports of the LDCs. This reluctance was strengthened by the growing consciousness from the late 1970s of the looming debt crisis facing many LDCs – a problem which they could only be expected to overcome by their own efforts if they continued to have access to OECD countries' markets on terms at least as favourable as those accorded by the latter to each other. In any event the industrialized countries were powerless to prevent the LDCs – and in particular the newly industrialized countries (NICs), which accounted for the lion's share of manufacturing growth in the Third World[7] – from taking over most of their former export markets outside the OECD area itself.

ADDING TO EXCESS CAPACITY

Thus it is more than ever apparent that the remedy of raising old-fashioned trade barriers against LDC exports offers little hope of alleviating the problem of growing competition, while at the same time holding few political attractions. Although there exists the possibility of world market cartelization of basic products such as steel – along the lines of the MFA for textiles – this seems unlikely to occur in a hurry or in other than the present piecemeal, bilateral fashion (see chapter 8). The alternative, in many countries, is to hold on in the hope either that world markets will resume their rapid growth or that the weaker producers – that is to say those with the least financial muscle – will gradually be forced to abandon production in the face of low prices and mounting losses. Yet, while the prolongation of the recession has at least forced the shelving of many major manufacturing projects under construction in LDCs, especially in Latin America, the shakeout has not been anything like as severe – in developed and developing countries alike – as the level of excess capacity would indicate is necessary. One major reason for this is that the financial institutions, mainly Western owned, which have financed these developments are by no means happy to see them written off – in the interests of rationalizing product markets – at the expense of their own balance sheets.

This in turn points to another significant element in the pattern of international market distortion which has made itself felt during the recession. This has been the increased tendency of OECD-based companies, banks and governments to encourage investments of all kinds in LDCs. In the first instance this was based on the need to 'recycle' the much-boosted oil revenues of the OPEC countries, which could only partly be absorbed by the latter themselves in the short run, while the sharp recession in the OECD countries – intensified by deflationary economic policies in most of them – meant that the demand for loan finance there dried up almost completely. Indeed many companies were on the contrary seeking to reduce their gearing – that is, the proportion of borrowing in their balance sheets – in response to the unexpected decline in their earnings growth prospects.

The belief that the LDCs offered a suitable outlet for the vast quantities of OPEC money which were flooding into the banks in 1974 and 1975 was thus based on the realization that – along with the centrally planned economies of Eastern Europe – they offered the only source of demand for such funds. At the same time their creditworthiness was thought to be considerably improved by the prospect that, as commodity exporters, many LDCs could expect to benefit from the boom in commodity prices which had begun before the oil price rise and was continuing in its wake – often in the naïve belief that exporters of commodities would in many cases be able to cartelize world markets for them in the manner of OPEC and thereby effect a permanent increase in their real price. This powerfully conditioned optimism – which in any case was at variance with the broader interests of the industrialized countries, which was to bring down inflation – was combined with a scarcely less questionable faith in the gilt-edged nature of sovereign debt. Such fantasies induced a great rash of lending to LDCs in the 1974-76 period – which the latter were only too willing to accept and which may be said to have laid the foundations of the debt crisis that was to follow the second oil 'shock' in 1979 and that we shall discuss later in this chapter.

Perhaps the most lasting effect of this burst of enthusiasm for lending to the Third World was that it greatly expanded the productive capacity of LDCs in several areas of heavy industry (such as chemicals, steel, shipbuilding and non-ferrous smelting) as well as mining and agro-industrial projects. Such initiatives responded to the long-standing desire of the LDCs for more industrialization – and in particular for an increase in their share of the value added to their commodity exports by means of a greater degree of local processing. For the equipment suppliers the main consideration was that these previously untapped markets provided an outlet for their products at a time when – as in the case of the banks – their OECD markets were contracting severely. Neither they nor the banks appear to have seriously considered the possibility that they might have been exacerbating what was already, in many sectors, a serious problem of global oversupply.

For their part OECD governments, the IMF and other international agencies were only too happy to support the process, which they saw as helping to avert the worst effects of the downturn pending what they expected to be an early resumption of the pre-1973 pattern of steady growth. Indeed this strong official

backing for the recycling process was probably the crucial ingredient behind the whole exercise, since it is difficult – if only with the
benefit of hindsight – to comprehend how financial institutions
could have conscientiously lent money for many of the capital
projects initiated in the LDCs in the mid-1970s unless they
believed their loans to be implicitly underwritten by one 'lender of
last resort' or another.

ECLIPSE OF THE PRICE MECHANISM

Indeed it is a measure of the extent to which interventionism was
entrenched in the international system by the early 1970s that the
one solution to the underlying imbalance of the world economy
which would have been most clearly indicated by the principles of
classical orthodoxy – a slump deep enough to squeeze out all the
uneconomic surplus capacity – was never seriously advocated by
any institution, government or political party. Thus, as demonstrated in chapter 5, even the Thatcher administration in Britain –
arguably the most avowedly committed of all major OECD
governments of recent years to the restoration of *laissez-faire*
principles – has consistently shrunk from exposing most of the
loss-making sectors of the British economy to the full rigours of the
marketplace. (Even where it has made some show of standing by
its belief in the virtues of the market – as in the case of shipbuilding
and to some extent of steel – it is clear that the government could
not have afforded to indulge its ideological tendencies without the
luxury of rising revenues from North Sea oil.) This general attitude
was, of course, largely conditioned by the 'economics of euphoria'
– according to which the underlying momentum of growth was
thought to be so unstoppable that demand was bound sooner or
later to catch up with excess supply – and by the unspoken feeling
that the consequences of a genuine shakeout would be too awful to
contemplate, both financially and politically. Moreover, the
longer governments forbore to impose market disciplines the more
catastrophic any such shakeout was bound to be. 'In the end, by
following the universal prescription that they must not allow
shocks to become disruptions, the Fed. and the Bank of England
create a situation where only a disruption can administer the
corrections that should come from shocks.'[8]

In other words the recession served to expose and yet also to underpin the most basic assumption of interventionist capitalism – that governments would in the last resort refuse to permit an economic collapse such as had occurred in the 1929-31. For, as shown in chapter 5, even a relatively peripheral incident such as the British property market collapse of 1973-74 was capable of shaking the whole national banking system so profoundly that a major financial upheaval (with potentially serious international repercussions) was only averted by timely intervention on the part of the Bank of England.

The far-reaching consequences of this momentous change in the basic mechanism of the market system were and still are scarcely perceived by the general public – a fact which may be ascribed as much to official reluctance to spell them out as to general bemusement at the complexities of international finance. This reluctance, it may be suspected, stems from a recognition that the development of the state's role as lender of last resort to the private sector has effectively demolished one of the central ideological tenets of free enterprise capitalism – the ultimate validity of the price mechanism as a basis for impartial resource allocation reflecting the expression of economic demands and needs. For, once it became clear that the verdicts of the market could in effect be overruled by governments and that this was happening on a more or less arbitrary basis, it might be supposed that, at the very least, such decisions and the affairs of the organizations which benefited from them would have to be made more subject to the principles of public accountability and scrutiny. Worse still, it could call in question the principal justification for high levels of private profit, namely that these are the proper reward for risk in an inevitably uncertain world. Concern at the danger of this contradiction becoming too glaring is even periodically expressed by such staunch defenders of the faith as the *Financial Times*. Commenting on the failure of many of the small businesses set up under the Thatcher government's Loan Guarantee Scheme (see chapter 5), it has suggested that at least the taxpayer, as the principal risk bearer, should have a share of the rewards of those state-assisted businesses which do make money.[9]

The possibility that such perceptions could eventually threaten the independence of action of private sector companies – multinational or otherwise – has clearly not escaped the leaders of business. Presumably indeed it is precisely because they are aware of their ideologically precarious position that many captains of industry and finance feel it necessary to continue stressing the virtues of being subject to the disciplines of the market and the desirability of *laissez-faire* as against the 'interference' which the business community has to endure from governments. No sector has been more shameless than the banking industry in its systematic denunciation of government regulation both in its own industry and in the economy generally, while accepting the ultimate protection of the state against the consequences of its own misjudgments. As a distinguished commentator on international monetary and financial questions succinctly put it, 'the banks cast critical eyes on [state intervention in] all but its original and most pervasive form, the support provided by the central bank to the banks themselves.'[10]

THE DEBT CRISIS

The vulnerability of the banks to such charges of double standards has increased with the unfolding of the international debt 'crisis', which has forced itself on the world's consciousness with steadily growing insistence since 1979, and particularly since Mexico's *de facto* declaration of insolvency in August 1982. The scale of the problem is reflected in the rise in the collective liabilities of the LDCs from some $200 billion in 1974 to around $800 billion by the beginning of 1984, with the certainty (at the time of writing) that it will continue to rise rapidly for the foreseeable future.

As suggested earlier, this financial disaster stems mainly from a combination of the improvidence of the international banks on the one hand and on the other of the desperate plight of many LDCs and manufacturing companies in the wake of the collapse of the post-war boom. However, it is only fair to point out that the lack of discipline induced by the 'lender of last resort' syndrome has also been reflected in the widespread corruption associated with much project finance. Thus it has been authoritatively reported that up to one third of Mexico's accumulated debt – which totalled over $70 billion in 1982 – never entered the country nor could be accounted for in terms of actual investment expenditure there, but instead went straight from the lending institutions to the offshore bank accounts of government officials and others involved in negotiating the contracts. Indeed almost anyone with first-hand experience of the implementation or evaluation of development projects in LDCs in recent years could cite numerous examples of similar misappropriation of funds, particularly in the shape of the provision by foreign suppliers of inappropriate and/or overpriced equipment.

Yet if there can be some difference of opinion as to the proper apportionment of blame for the LDC debt problem, there can be no disputing the fact that a politically acceptable solution to it is not remotely in prospect. The official view is that the countries affected can be restored to solvency by the imposition of 'stabilization' programmes of varying degrees of severity designed by the IMF. Yet such policies, unpopular as they are in the LDCs themselves, often amount to little more than a weak genuflection in the direction of orthodoxy – with little sign that those who insist on the need for such austerity really believe that it can be enforced, even if they are convinced of its efficacy. Thus the imposition of such an IMF package on Brazil in 1983 – in the teeth of fierce domestic opposition – has at the time of writing failed to bring down the country's inflation rate of over 150 per cent a year or to enable it to pay the interest on its foreign debt without recourse to further borrowings. The former point suggests that the requirement for real wage cuts – a key demand of the IMF which was conceded only after a major political crisis – has not in fact been implemented in a large part of the economy. (This suspicion has been confirmed by the announcement, in September 1984, that the legislation enforcing wage cuts is to be repealed less than 12 months after it was enacted, without any apparent objection from the IMF – in spite, or perhaps because of the fact that inflation was by then actually higher – at 190 per cent – than at the time it was introduced.) This apparent pattern of stern talk combined with lax enforcement suggests that the role of the IMF increasingly has more to do with public relations than with the application of a consistent code of discipline. This is certainly consistent (in the author's experience) with the approach being adopted in an equally insolvent country in Africa – the Sudan. Even in the aftermath of the 1979 oil shock the local representative of the IMF in Khartoum, while insisting on the need for austerity and 'structural adjustments' to overcome the country's growing external imbalance, was at pains to proclaim his confidence in its ability to pay off its debts by 1990. Given that Sudan's debt service ratio (annual debt servicing costs as a percentage of export earnings) had already reached 40 per cent by 1979, this optimism seemed so studied as to suggest that the IMF saw its primary role as being to bolster the confidence of the international banking community sufficiently to ensure that old loans were not called in too promptly and that new ones would be forthcoming on reasonable terms – in spite of all the evidence indicating a more pessimistic scenario. At all events the scepticism aroused by these rosy projections has been fully justified by subsequent events, which have seen Sudan's foreign debt burden rise to the point where by 1982 the theoretical debt service obligations were well over 50 per cent of export earnings, whereas actual repayments of interest and principal amounted to only 7.5 per cent of export earnings.

On the other hand it cannot be said that permissiveness is now all-pervading or that the IMF is not anxious at least to give the impression that it will insist on the application of financial rigour by a government before giving it the seal of approval which will ensure the maintenance or renewal of lending by the multinational banks. For

'to keep its standing in the banking community, the Fund has to show that it is not prepared to be cowed by demands from the debtors for easier terms. In the short term it might be easier for the IMF to gain an agreement with Brazil by accepting... that the terms now proposed are too harsh. In the long run, however, its authority as a disciplinarian would suffer and banks would no longer trust it to insist on the right austerity measures as a back-up for billions of dollars in new loans.'[11]

Yet despite this unbending public stance there can be little doubt that the severity of the IMF's approach both to framing an austerity package and to its subsequent enforcement varies in the light of political considerations, even if it sometimes only relaxes its conditions in the face of bloodshed – as occurred in Egypt following the food riots of January 1977. To this extent the Fund cannot be said to be pursuing a wholly principled and consistent policy, but rather is simply following the line of least resistance in the hope that this will enable the world banking system to survive ideologically as well as financially unscathed.

The delicacy of this task is all the greater in view of the growing popular awareness in many LDCs (especially in Latin America) of the true origins of their national indebtedness and the widespread feeling that there is neither political justice nor economic logic in trying to compel the mass of the population in these countries – already living at or below the level of absolute poverty – to assume the burden of repayment. For if much of the huge indebtedness of Brazil, Mexico and the rest was incurred as a result of high level mismanagement and corruption – often by governments which were clearly not representative of their population in any but the most theoretical sense – it is small wonder that many people in the countries affected feel no moral obligation to pay the price of such maladministration. This sentiment clearly lay behind the demand of the democratically elected government of Argentina, which assumed office under President Alfonsin in December 1983, to renegotiate the terms under which its $43 billion foreign debt had been rescheduled by the outgoing – and notoriously corrupt – military junta. Moreover, the determination of debtor countries to resist the demands of financial orthodoxy can only be increased by such events as the decision by the Reagan administration in 1984 effectively to nationalise the Continental Illinois Bank (eighth largest in the US) rather than see it collapse as a result of its own ill-advised lending policies.

Equally, many of the 'stabilization' measures imposed by the IMF appear designed to damage the medium- and long-term economic prospects of debtor countries, even though they may assist debt recovery in the short run. Not even this objective is served by certain public expenditure cuts – as in the case of the withdrawal of subsidies for farmers and exporters announced in Brazil's 1984 budget, which will inevitably tend to have an adverse impact on the all-important current balance of payments. Similarly the ending or curtailment of internal price controls or subsidies – practices which are particularly abhorrent to the IMF – can have the effect of boosting inflation, something which also tends to be fuelled by the currency devaluations they likewise tend to insist upon.

INCREASING RESORT TO BARTER

While the indebtedness of the Third World remains a conundrum which is apparently without a solution that would be consistent with the principles of market economics, its consequences for the pattern of world trade and production are becoming progressively more significant. Its direct impact on trade is most obviously reflected in the decline in the imports of LDCs, which is the inevitable result of having to make available a bigger proportion of their foreign exchange earnings for debt repayment. Perhaps more important in its consequences for the long-term evolution of the world trading system, however, is the growth in barter or, as it is known in the modern economists' vernacular, 'countertrade'. This is an approach to managing international trade which has, of course, been traditionally associated with the centrally planned economies of Comecon. Yet since the late 1970s many LDCs have had increasing recourse to it, as an ever greater number of them have seen their hard currency foreign exchange reserves severely depleted and have thus found that barter is the only means of paying for essential imports. It is naturally a particularly attractive device for facilitating trade between LDCs which are in similar straitened circumstances on their external account. Thus for example Brazil, which has been a prominent exponent of the practice, has recently bartered its manufactured products for Mexican oil to a value of hundreds of millions of dollars.

At the same time LDCs which are much further from bankruptcy than Brazil or Mexico, such as Malaysia and Indonesia, are insisting on barter deals as a means to promote their manufactured exports, with a view to reducing their traditional dependence on exports of primary commodities – and also in some cases to redressing their trade balance with those countries with which they are in significant deficit. Indonesia has even tried to use the barter weapon as a lever for prizing open the door which it regards as unfairly barring its access to OECD textile markets, refusing – in one recent instance – to award a major engineering contract to a British group unless these restrictions were relaxed. In such ways exporters based in the OECD are also finding that they must increasingly be prepared to accept payment in kind if they wish to do business with LDCs.

The extent to which this trend towards barter is gathering momentum is shown by a recent authoritative estimate that the share of world trade accounted for by countertrade rose from under 15 per cent in 1979 to nearly 30 per cent in 1982 – almost trebling in absolute terms.[12] Once again it is striking that the GATT Secretariat has apparently remained silent in the face of this explosion, perhaps because to point out that it contravenes the spirit of the GATT's rules on non-discrimination would simply serve to emphasize the growing irrelevance of the GATT.

AN INADEQUATE SHAKE-OUT

The LDCs' mounting debt problems are also an important factor in perpetuating the chronic crisis of overcapacity in the world economy – a crisis which is rendered all the more intractable by social pressures against closures and rising unemployment in OECD countries. Although the level of capacity is difficult to measure in many industries, there is evidence in virtually all traditional areas of manufacturing of a chronic failure to adjust capacity levels to stagnant or falling levels of demand. The most striking instance of this failure is perhaps in shipbuilding, where the level of world order books declined from a peak of 133 million gross tons in March 1974 to only 25 million tons in March 1979, after which it rose slightly to around 35 million tons in 1982 and has continued to stagnate at around that level since. In the face of this drop in demand of over 70 per cent the Japanese industry (which accounts for over half of world production) has cut capacity – according to its own estimates – by only 35 per cent, while Britain and other major shipbuilding countries in Western Europe have experienced cuts of up to 50 per cent. Against this, however, productive capacity has been expanded sharply in a number of LDCs (notably South Korea and Brazil), which together with the growing industries in Southern and Eastern Europe (Spain, Yugoslavia and Poland) have now replaced West Germany, Britain and Sweden as the main shipbuilding nations after Japan.

The net effect of these developments is that world shipbuilding capacity in 1984 is probably no more than 20 per cent below the level of ten years earlier in spite of the 70 per cent fall in orders. (The gap has, it is true, been partly filled by construction work for the rapidly expanding offshore oil and gas industry, though much of this business – which requires a far more sophisticated technology – is going to purpose-built facilities close to the oil fields concerned.) Significantly this imbalance has come about despite discreet efforts to cartelize the market – or at least to share the burden of capacity cutbacks – organized under the aegis of the OECD (of which South Korea, Brazil and Poland are not members and thus not subject to the pressure which is exerted on the other major producers). In short, if the world shipbuilding market has effectively defied efforts to subject it to cartelization and 'managed' trade, it is not altogether for want of trying on the part of most of the industry and of the governments concerned. Their failure to do so stems not only from the lack of a truly comprehensive cartel structure but also, as in other industries, from a persistent tendency to be over-optimistic about the prospects for market recovery. At the same time, the possibility of continuing to resist the logic of the market and of maintaining capacity well above economically viable levels has been increased by the fact that the vast majority of yards in Western Europe have been taken into public ownership since 1974, while in Japan and South Korea shipbuilding yards or companies are in most cases part of diversified heavy engineering groups, which makes it possible both to conceal the true level of profit or loss derived from shipbuilding and to cross-subsidize it from more profitable activities if need be.

An equally telling illustration of this refusal to bow to the inexorable pressures of the marketplace is provided by post-1973 trends in the West European plastics industry, which like the petrochemicals sector in general has had to withstand a particularly steep rise in the price of its petroleum-based raw materials as well as stagnant demand. In 1973, at the end of a long period of sustained annual growth in demand of 10-20 per cent, the rate of capacity utilization in the production of basic plastics in Western Europe stood at upwards of 85 per cent. By the time of the second oil crisis in 1979 this had slumped to 65 per cent in the case of low density polyethylene and as little as 50 percent in that of polypropylene. Since then, despite a steady closure of petrochemical plants in the region, overcapacity in many products has remained close to 40 per cent, while losses in the European plastics and petrochemical sector totalled over $3 billion in 1981 and 1982 (losses which could only be sustained thanks to *de facto* cross-subsidization from within the groups concerned).

This failure to respond more quickly to the recession is partly a reflection of the inherent rigidities of an industry where individual plants are extremely large and expensive (so that reluctance to write them off is correspondingly great) and partly also, once again, of chronic over-optimism as to recovery prospects. It has also been compounded by the belief – for which there was some justification until recently – that part of the trouble stemmed from unfair competition on the part of US producers who benefited from subsidized feedstock prices. At the same time resistance to closures has also been politically inspired in some cases – notably in France and Italy, where the industry has been seen as of key importance in the economic development of otherwise relatively deprived regions.

The problem of overcapacity in the petrochemicals/plastics sector is, moreover, certain to be aggravated before the end of the 1980s by the commissioning of substantial new petrochemical plants in Middle Eastern oil producing countries – particularly Saudi Arabia – most of whose total planned capacity is certain to be surplus to local requirements and thus offloaded on to world markets. Indeed the establishment of petrochemical industries in these and other OPEC countries has been undertaken precisely in order to provide an alternative source of foreign exchange earnings against the day when oil reserves dwindle. Moreover, the Saudi authorities have been at pains to emphasise that, contrary to what has been widely believed in the West, these new plants should be extremely competitive, incorporating as they do the very latest technology and using low-cost ethane gas as a feedstock. What they have failed to point out is that the pricing of this gas – at only around 10 per cent of what the average European petrochemical producer would pay for its feedstock – incorporates a massive subsidy, since it takes no account of what it could be sold for at export. (It has been hinted that this apparent refusal to apply the textbook method of export parity pricing is to be justified in terms of the principles of 'Islamic economics'. If so, it would be interesting to have an official GATT view on whether this is compatible with its rules.)

This development is a classic illustration of the way in which uncoordinated investment plans, motivated at least as much by 'strategic' considerations as by criteria of profitability, are tending to perpetuate imbalances in world markets. It also demonstrates the potentially serious conflict between OECD and LDC interests as countries struggle to increase or, in the OECD case, maintain their share of a stagnant world market. Likewise the reaction of the oil and chemical multinationals to the Saudi push into petrochemicals is further evidence of the tendency of major suppliers – identified earlier in this chapter – to respond to the chronic depression of world markets by seeking to join forces with each other or with new market entrants in both production and marketing operations, thereby limiting competition. In this case Exxon, Mitsubishi and Mobil have taken a stake in the new plants in Saudi Arabia – and are widely expected to be followed by European-based oil and chemical giants (perhaps linking up with new producers elsewhere in the Gulf) – on the basis that they will be responsible for marketing the bulk of the exports.

As excess capacity has become an enduring symptom of the recession common to virtually every established sector of manufacturing, the methods of coping with it have also become to a large extent institutionalized. Nowhere is this more evident than in Japan, which – contrary to popular belief in the West – has not escaped the impact of the recession and has seen its unemployment rate double since 1973 to almost 3 per cent of the labour force (admittedly still much lower than elsewhere in the OECD). The government, through MITI, makes no secret of its efforts to mobilise the cooperative spirit of companies in the growing number of industries (including machine tools, motor cycles, photographic equipment and typewriters) which have become the victims of their own tendency to expand too fast, usually with a view to forming some kind of 'crisis cartel' and thus eliminating excessive competition among Japanese suppliers for saturated markets at home and abroad.

In many industries, moreover, Japan is faced with the threat of increased competition from newly industrialized countries (NICs) – especially those in its own region such as Hong Kong, South Korea, Singapore and Taiwan. Collectively they have already long surpassed Japan in importance as textile exporters and have made substantial inroads into its share of world markets for shipbuilding, watches and consumer electronics. The likelihood that this process will intensify and extend to other sectors such as steel and motor vehicles has led the major Japanese firms to abandon their traditional reluctance to invest abroad and has thus induced them to begin transforming themselves into multinational companies – a process which has been further aided by resistance to ever increasing Japanese exports to other OECD countries and the consequent need to establish local manufacturing capacity (whether or not on a joint venture basis) to secure access to the local market.

IDEOLOGICAL CONTRADICTIONS

The success of the NICs and other Third World countries in gaining a greater share of international trade in manufactures, while far from sufficient to make the achievement of the UNIDO target of a 25 per cent share of world markets for LDCs likely by the end of the century, has none the less caused enough concern among developed countries to inspire some imitation of their methods in promoting investment. In particular the practice of establishing duty free zones or freeports – where all imports are exempt from duty provided that they are re-exported in one form or another rather than being marketed locally – has become a popular method of taking a leaf out of Hong Kong's book. In consequence freeports have proliferated throughout the world since the early 1970s and according to some estimates already handled some 10 per cent of world trade by 1983. The concept has attracted much interest in the EEC, where West Germany, the Netherlands and France have pioneered the practice – now to be followed by the UK with no fewer than six freeports.

What seems astonishing about this development is that few of its supporters appear to have recognized that resort to this method of export subsidization by all countries is bound to be a zero sum game in terms of the public interest. Less surprising perhaps is contradiction in an avowed supporter of undistorted free trade such as the Thatcher administration initiating a move to increased subsidization in a way which is clearly contrary to the spirit of the GATT. This attitude is in line with the traditional difficulty experienced by pro-business interests in recognizing that a discriminatory exemption from tax is equivalent to a subsidy. Still less remarkable, in view of its past failure to come to grips with the use of tax concessions as subsidies, is the fact that the vogue for freeports seems to have raised not a squeak of protest from the GATT secretariat.

This particular blind spot is but one instance of a striking tendency on the part of many avowed free market enthusiasts to adopt inconsistent positions when faced with the conflicting social and commercial pressures of the recession. Thus in Britain, despite an undoubted reversion in the weight of establishment thinking towards crude neo-classical economic ideas, all but the most hard-bitten ideologues seem conscious of the continuing need to combat unemployment and maintain or restore an acceptable minimum standard of living. This means that, while advocating a reduction in the real cost of labour to the mystical 'market-clearing' level as a cure for unemployment, many devotees of the marketplace recognize the political danger of seeking to depress wages too far below the poverty line – in the event that market-clearing rates of pay, if they could be shown to exist at all, proved to be below that line.

This dilemma has led some of the leading apostles of Mrs Thatcher's 'new consensus' into another contradictory posture. For on the one hand they advocate lower government expenditure and lower real wages as a means to promoting economic recovery and fuller employment; yet at the same time they assert that, since the level of wages which will induce employers to take on more staff is below the poverty line, the government must provide a 'safety net' whereby wages from employment are made up to a tolerable income level – whether through the social security system or in some other form – if it really wants more people in jobs.[13] The fact that the latter proposal runs counter to the former by requiring an increase in public spending does not seem to trouble many of its advocates, who see it mainly as a possible device for overcoming political opposition to the abolition of Wages Councils – the bodies guaranteeing statutory minimum rates of pay in certain industries where workers are poorly organized. Still less do they seem to appreciate that what they are in effect calling for is state subsidization of labour costs, or that many people might conclude that they are hiding their desire for ever greater state support under a cloak of pious rhetoric on the plight of the unemployed and low paid.

Yet amid the ideological confusion and double standards this debate highlights a central dilemma facing the British government as it seeks to grapple with the economic crisis. For, just as the potential consequences of applying classical *laissez-faire* logic to the financial markets are seen as too awful to contemplate, the prospect of a return to the world of the Poor Law and the workhouse – institutions whose dismantling in the 1920s and 1930s was largely the work of Conservative governments – is in the last resort equally unacceptable to all but the most extreme right-wing ideologues.

If this is true of Britain it is almost certainly no less so of other West European countries which have come to insist on a reasonable level of social security. In the United States – where the political commitment to 'welfare' has always been more tenuous – the position is evidently somewhat different. Indeed those who support the view that cutting real wages is the most appropriate, if not the only, cure for unemployment, like to point to the example of the US, where a degree of wage cutting has indeed been accompanied by a substantial rise in the numbers in work in the 1980s – compared with a fall in the EEC. However, the implied moral – that European countries could achieve the same sort of rise in employment, and a corresponding drop in unemployment, by adopting the same kind of 'flexibility' with regard to wage rates, rests on a rather shaky basis. In particular, it ignores the fact that employment has been rising much faster in the United States compared with Europe throughout the post-war period, despite the fact that average US wage rates and incomes have been higher than those of virtually every European country, while its productivity has grown consistently more slowly than that of Western Europe taken as a whole ever since 1965.[14]

This seeming paradox is largely attributable to the fact that the United States has for long been both much less dependent on foreign trade than European countries (exports account for only 7 per cent of gross national product compared with an average of over 25 per cent for the EEC countries) and has, partly for that reason, been far more effectively protected against it. (The reason for this is that because the US has not hitherto felt a strong need to export it has not had to make its industry any more competitive than is necessary to hold down imports to an acceptable level, something which it has been well able to do with the aid of its above

average de facto levels of protection – both tariff and non-tariff).[15]
At the same time it is seldom recognized that the United States is
both a far less socially and economically homogeneous country
than the EEC taken as a whole (even though it is a more integrated
market) and contains significant pockets of population – including
many recent immigrants from Mexico, Central America and the
Caribbean – with living standards and expectations more typical of
LDCs than of industrialized countries. This 'reserve army' of
labour undoubtedly accounts for a good deal of the growth in US
employment in the 1980s, as well as for the fact that expansion has
been most marked in the Southern and Western states, where
there is the heaviest concentration of relatively deprived groups.

Yet while this has permitted a continued rise in employment, it
has arguably been at the expense of the long-term competitiveness
of the US economy. For it seems improbable that any OECD
country will in the long run be able to compete in labour-intensive
forms of manufacturing with the NICs, so that ultimately US
industry will have to choose the road of high technology and high
capital intensity – at the price of a major shake-out of labour – if it
is to be competitive in world markets, or even its own market. The
need to make this choice will be all the more compelling to the
extent that the country's dependence on foreign trade – which has
been increasing steadily since the 1960s, albeit from a very low
level – becomes much greater in the future.

Perhaps because it is conscious of this long-term vulnerability
the US government has started to show signs of being more
determined than ever before to maintain US leadership in
technology as the key to its continued economic dominance of the
Western World. It is true that, seen in terms of the world-wide
strength of US-controlled multinational companies, the country's
economic power is still formidable, particularly in the all-
important field of computers, where the supremacy of IBM is if
anything more marked than ever despite intensive Japanese efforts
to challenge it. Yet there is clearly a contrast between this strength
in corporate terms and the relative weakness of the US economy
within its national frontiers. Official anxiety on the latter point is
doubtless all the greater in view of the country's increasing, and
evidently structural, balance of payments deficit. It may even have
occurred to some Americans that this weakness at home may in

some senses be the product of their corporate strength abroad, since US multinationals' large share of many world markets is not necessarily of any direct benefit to the national balance of payments and is certainly a negative influence on the level of US direct exports. For the ability of these companies to supply so many markets from their overseas subsidiaries naturally tends to mean that their home-based operations are excluded from many potential export markets.

Equally, it is starting to be recognized that this structure of multinational production makes it all too easy for technology developed in the US (mainly at the taxpayer's expense) to be used to give other countries a competitive edge in manufacturing or other sectors. It is such preoccupations which may well lie behind the Reagan administration's attempt to develop what appears to be a new weapon for its protectionist armoury, namely restriction of the transfer of technology developed in the US, although the professed reason for this policy is a concern lest it should become available to the Soviet bloc – to the strategic disadvantage of the West.

It is, of course, true that much of the US government's support for research and development programmes has been for military purposes in the first instance. It may therefore seem entirely proper that it should seek to restrict access to it to those countries it considers its military allies. The problem is that a great deal of military-related technology also has civilian applications, so that the boundary between technology which is strategic (in the narrowest sense) and that which is not is often difficult if not impossible to draw. The only international machinery for trying to do so is the Coordinating Committee for Multilateral Export Controls (CoCom), whose membership is roughly coterminous with that of the NATO alliance. Yet its evident ineffectiveness has induced the United States to try and apply legal sanctions of its own on the export to the Soviet bloc by other Western countries of products incorporating components or technology originating in the US which it regards as sensitive. This in turn has provoked complaints of arbitrariness and discrimination in the US application of such restrictions. It has even caused the leading British computer manufacturer, ICL, to suggest that the US is employing strategic arguments as a cover for what is really an attempt to restrict freedom of technology transfer and thus maintain or increase US dominance in the fields concerned – with obvious implications for international trade competitiveness.

This suggestion is one which US officials have scarcely bothered to deny, even though their desire to prevent Warsaw Pact countries from gaining access to military-related technology is no doubt sincere. Indeed one of them complained to a seminar on East-West relations held in Vienna in April 1984 that 'there is simply too much diffusion of technology. Semi-conductors, to take one example, are now made in some 40 countries throughout the world.'[16] This statement clearly implies a feeling that high technology – like nuclear weapons – could be a dangerous weapon in the wrong hands, though it is also consistent with the ICL thesis that one of the dangers which the US wishes to avoid from the dissemination of advanced technology is the threat to US control over its commercial application.

Yet perhaps more significant and inimical to this policy than the opposition of the United States' trading partners and allies is that of its own multinationals, whose interests are in this instance also at variance with those of the US government. In particular, IBM sees US government attempts to impose restrictions on the use or resale of its computers – even when these are manufactured outside the US – as potentially very damaging to its ability to conduct its world-wide operations independently. Indeed the company has already expressed concern at the effect of such interference on its position in the EEC market, where it has lately been at pains to cultivate the image of being as much a European company as an American one – to such effect that there is even a possibility that it will be invited to participate in the ESPRIT project designed by the Community to enhance its collective capability in computer technology.

This incident has not only demonstrated the near impossibility of isolating the impact of state intervention in the military field from that in the civilian economy – especially when it is so often the conscious intention of governments to cross-subsidize the latter through the former. It has also provided a graphic illustration of the extent to which the industrialized market economies have – largely through the agency of the multinationals – become locked into a structure of international trade which is at least as much collaborative as competitive. As suggested earlier in this chapter, this is the result of the pressures of recession pushing governments, financial institutions and industrial companies into various acts of cartelization, merger and subsidization – usually in a quite disparate and *ad hoc* fashion – aimed at neutralizing the pitiless demands of market forces. The problem is that by failing openly to recognize the nature of this process – and by refusing to try and put it on a more rationally coordinated basis – the leaders of Western nations are helping to perpetuate the very instability which they seek to escape through their isolated response to it.

NOTES

(1) Cf. E.F. Denison, *Why Growth Rates Differ*. Washington. Brookings Institution 1967.

(2) And indeed may be said to have evolved from the 1962 Short-term and Long-term Arrangements on Cotton Textiles (see chapter 2).

(3) The most far-reaching instances – concerning steel – is the subject of a separate case study in the next chapter.

(4) The Japanese are by no means viewed as the sole source of salvation, as is shown by similar links between the Swedish car firms Volvo and Saab with, respectively, Renault and Fiat/Lancia.

(5) Consideration of the state's role in relation to the development of new technology leads one to speculate about the way this technology might have developed in the absence of state involvement. It is certainly arguable that without governments forcing the pace the level of resources devoted to R & D would have been much more a function of the need to respond to demand for commercial applications of it – and thus much lower than it has actually been, entailing a slower growth of technological change – whereas in reality the technology seems often to have been developed in advance of commercial uses for it being identified (e.g. lasers).

(6) Cf. Cambridge University Department of Applied Economics. *Economic Policy Review*, March 1978. It was their belief, based on the observed trends of the 1950s and 1960s, that there was no evidence of 'technological unemployment' – that is, of any long-term change in the statistical relationship between output and productivity growth.

(7) Including Brazil, Mexico, Hong Kong, Singapore, South Korea, Taiwan and India.

(8) M. Mayer, *The Bankers*. London. W.H. Allen 1976.

(9) Heads they win, tails we lose, 5 April 1984.

(10) F. Hirsch, The Ideological Underlay of Inflation, in F. Hirsch and J. Goldthorpe (eds), *The Political Economy of Inflation*. Oxford. Martin Robertson 1978.

(11) Why the IMF is keeping up the pressure, *Financial Times*, 6 September 1983.

(12) Business Trend Analysts, *The World of Countertrade*. New York 1984.

(13) This was the burden, for instance, of the argument advanced by Mr Walter Goldsmith, Director-General of the Institute of Directors, on BBC Television's *Panorama* on 19 December 1983.

(14) To some extent also the rise in US unemployment, particularly since 1982, has been a statistical quirk, since it conceals a substantial switch by employers from a full-time to a part-time labour force.

(15) An example of this is the US shipbuilding industry, which although quite large in international terms exports virtually nothing. It is kept in business solely by virtue of contracts for the US Navy and by the simple requirement, enshrined in the Jones Act, that at least half of all the country's seaborne trade must be carred in vessels built in the United States.

(16) Mr Olin Wethington, US Deputy Trade Under-Secretary, quoted in the *Financial Times*, 4 April 1984.

CHAPTER 8

From Chaos to Cartel – the Case of World Steel

A 1976 United Nations report on the world steel industry affirmed that

'Potential for growth exists in the iron and steel sectors of both industrialized and developing countries, as does potential for cooperation in this area between developed and developing countries, for whereas the former dispose of the necessary capital, know-how and technology, the latter have raw material in abundance, the labour to mine it, processing sites relatively free of environmental problems, and vast markets for the final products. It is a situation that underscores the fact that the modern world has become an interdependent entity in which countries and groups of countries must consult and cooperate with one another for the common good.'[1]

This quotation is not untypical, as some readers will perhaps recognize, of the visionary tone of many United Nations reports on the possibilities of world ecomomic development which were compiled in the 1960s and early 1970s. What makes this particular document remarkable, however, is that it was produced fully three years after what is now generally recognized as the end of the post-war boom, and yet apparently refuses to take any cognizance of this harsh reality. Its authors thus saw no reason for abandoning the boom-time forecasting technique of extrapolating past high growth rates into the indefinite future. The fact that world steel output had actually fallen between 1973 and 1975 was doubtless, in their eyes, simply a short-term, cyclical deviation from an ineluctable trend of rapid growth – the existence of which was thought to be evident from the fact that world output had doubled between 1958 and 1971. It is instructive to compare their projections with the observed reality of the early 1980s (table 8.1).

Table 8.1
World Crude Steel Output – UNIDO forecasts compared with reality (million tonnes)

	EEC, Japan, USA	LDCs*	Other	Total
1970	350	22	224	596
1981 (UNIDO forecast)	405	65	405	910
1981 (actual)	337	59	311	707

* *Excluding China*

Sources: OECD, *The Steel Market in 1980*; B. Keeling, *The World Steel Industry – Structure and Prospects in the 1980s*. London. *The Economist* Intelligence Unit 1983.

CONDITIONED OPTIMISM AND LDC AMBITIONS

It is not our purpose to pillory the failings of those whose unenviable lot is to make their living as economic forecasters. Rather it is to help explain the continuing – and even increasing – imbalance between supply and demand which has been manifest in steel, as in other world industrial markets, during the recession. In this context what is significant about these projections is not so much that they resulted from defective methodology as that they were the product of a 'growth psychology' which was both a cause and a result of the clamour for higher living standards in developed and developing countries alike. Seen from this standpoint they were clearly a response to the several hopes and aspirations of the different interested groups of steel producing countries. For it was quite obvious in the aftermath of the 1973-74 downturn, and in the face of growing LDC demands for a greater share of world output and trade in manufactures, that the perceived needs of both industrialized and less developed countries could not both be met without a resumption of economic growth at least as rapid as had prevailed before the recession.

Indeed the UNIDO report just cited was commissioned for the very purpose of exploring the likely consequences of implementing the Lima Declaration commitment of raising LDCs' share of world industrial production to 25 per cent by the year 2000. It is therefore probably reasonable to suppose that the authors had a particular bias in favour of finding that the fulfilment of this target in the case of steel was consistent with continued growth in the output of industrialized coutries as well as of LDCs. It is in any case only fair to point out that most of the ambitious expansion plans which so many steel producers, in both developed and developing countries, embarked upon in the 1970s were undertaken without any prompting from UNIDO – and indeed in advance of the publication of the report quoted above – but rather at the behest of decision makers who were quite as wilfully blind to the realities of the world economy as the UNIDO forecasters. Indeed there was unquestionably a general reluctance – reinforced by the conditions resulting from years of sustained growth – to contemplate the possibility that the recession might prove durable, if only because to adopt such a hypothesis would have entailed making politically unacceptable choices. It would moreover have meant going against the prevailing belief that not only was growth sustainable over the long period but that the beneficiaries from the continued expansion would be those who invested heavily in modern plant, which usually meant in high capacity units, given the assumed benefits of 'economies of scale'.

Such was undoubtedly the conventional wisdom in Britain in the early 1970s when the Heath government decided on a major expansion plan for the state-owned British Steel Corporation. Under this plan, which was announced in 1973, the Corporation was to raise its annual output from around 23 million tonnes in 1972 to a minimum of 28 million tonnes by 1980-81. In fact this objective was regarded as far too modest by the Steel Committee of the Trades Union Congress, which managed to persuade the government to adopt a target range, with an upper limit of 36 million tonnes a year – an implied rate of growth even higher than projected by UNIDO. Optimism was scarcely less extreme in other European countries where similar expansion schemes were initiated in the same period. It is true that the market appraisals justifying these decisions were for the most part made before the collapse of the boom, when many major steel using industries – notably construction and shipbuilding – were also experiencing frenzied expansion. They were thus made without the benefit of the limited hindsight open to UNIDO in 1976, by which time steel output in the EEC had fallen back from its peak of 156.5 million tonnes in 1974 to under 135 million tonnes. Yet few would have strongly dissented from the UNIDO view that this downturn – which roughly paralleled that in the world steel industry as a whole – was other than an unusually sharp cyclical adjustment, and certainly none foresaw that it would drop to as little as 108 million tonnes (over 30 per cent below the 1974 peak) by 1983.

Eagerness to believe in forecasts of continued or renewed rapid growth in demand for steel was, if anything, even greater in the case of the LDCs. In fact this attitude considerably predated the Lima Declaration, since the establishment of some form of steel industry has traditionally been regarded by LDCs as indispensable to any country with serious pretensions to being industrialized. Moreover, in those numerous LDCs with both iron ore and coal reserves their exploitation for local steel production is typically seen as a natural priority, almost regardless of cost and market considerations. Thus in Nigeria plans for the development of a national steel industry – under consideration ever since independence – envisage the outlay of at least $7 billion during the 1980s to create a productive capacity of 3.5 million tonnes by 1990 (about half local consumption projected for that date, though slightly above the 1983 level). Yet even before construction of most of this capacity had started it was openly conceded by the authorities that the industry could only be competitive with the aid of massive and prolonged government subsidies, even if all the technical question marks over it – concerning the quality of local iron ore and coal and possible transport difficulties – were to be satisfactorily resolved. Such determined defiance of apparent market logic undoubtedly helps to explain why the number of steel producing countries in the world rose from 32 in 1950 to 76 in 1982.

AN ALLIANCE OF THE IMPRUDENT AND THE UNSCRUPULOUS

But if the enthusiasm for such projects on the part of LDCs was often the expression of an irrational fetishism, that of the bankers, aid donors and suppliers of plant and equipment in the industrialized countries stemmed from a perversion of economic rationality which was no less reprehensible. The tendency of developed country suppliers of capital goods to try and sell their wares to LDCs which do not need them, cannot use them and/or cannot afford them is a phenomenon which was familiar enough before the upheaval of 1973. As mentioned in chapter 7, however, once manufacturing investment in the OECD countries effectively dried up with the onset of recession, the competition among these suppliers – fully aided and abetted by both their governments and the banks – to win orders from the Third World intensified dramatically. It would certainly be unfair to say that there was in no case any attempt to relate the scale of investment projects to a realistic assessment of their potential sales, or that no account was taken of the technical suitability of much of the equipment sold. Yet there can be little doubt that these questions were thought by far too many supplying firms – and their backers – to be of secondary importance to that of the creditworthiness of the buyer, although even this was often taken for granted on the basis of bland assumptions about sovereign debt or of effective guarantees from the supplier's own government.

One factor which helps to explain the particularly chaotic pattern of the spread of steel production among LDCs was the virtual absence of any influence on the part of multinational companies over the scale and location of investment and production in this particular sector. For although the steel giants of the OECD (such as US Steel, Bethlehem, Nippon Steel and Thyssen) frequently participate in overseas mining ventures to assure their supplies of raw materials, it is rare for them to have a controlling, or even a minority, interest in steel manufacturing enterprises outside their own country. Quite why this should be so is not obvious, although it may be that their possible interest has been pre-empted by the determination of so many countries to establish steel production before the market was large enough to make it justifiable in commercial terms – a point which is underlined by the fact that the vast majority of steel producing enterprises in LDCs are in fact wholly or largely state-owned. Equally, a reason why it may have been more difficult to impose on steel the kind of market control which is possible in, say, motor cars or detergents is the fact that it is an 'intermediate' good not an end-product whose qualities can be readily differentiated as between one manufacturer and another, and as such is not susceptible to the power of marketing – the supreme strength of multinationals. Nor is it, like another form of semi-finished manufacture which is dominated by multinationals – petrochemicals – based on a cartelized supply of raw materials or a highly sophisticated technology whose diffusion can be relatively easily restricted. Thus in a sense the world steel market has more of the charateristics of a commodity market even though it is a manufactured product, a fact which is reflected in the great volatility of prices obtainable on the international market.

But if there has been a lack of interest on the part of OECD-based steel manufacturers in participating in LDC production ventures in this sector, the same could not be said of suppliers of plant and machinery from the industrialized countries. As with chemical plant suppliers – which are often the same firms – these companies have, in the absence of new orders closer to home (except in Japan), redoubled their efforts to win contracts under the programmes for rapid expansion of steel industries in the Third World, notably in NICs such as Mexico, Brazil, India and South Korea. In this instance at least it would be somewhat unfair to accuse them of having encouraged their clients in reckless expansion in contradiction of authoritative advice as to market growth prospects. For, as we have seen, official wisdom (as represented by UNIDO) held until relatively recently that the long-term growth prospects were such as to justify accelerated expansion of capacity by LDCs. On the other hand, even since it has become obvious – following the second oil shock in 1979 and the onset of the Third World debt crisis – that demand for steel was falling far short of earlier projections and that any new capacity was bound to be surplus to world requirements, plant exporters have been avidly competing for new business. In this their resolve has been stiffened by the usually unwavering support of both multinational banks and their own governments – the latter giving encouragement with subsidized credit insurance and other subventions.

CAPACITY STILL GROWING IN THE RECESSION

It is true that the development of such new projects often appears viable in narrowly commercial terms, even if the subsidization of credit is clearly questionable. Thus for example the announcement in 1983 of a plan for another 2.7 million tonne integrated steel works to be established in South Korea may well make sense in terms of a comparison of its production costs with those of other countries and its consequent theoretical ability to make inroads in export markets – although the main sufferers to date from its expansion, the US steel producers, claim that it is subsidized. Likewise a plan by Indonesia (also announced in 1983) to establish a plant to produce 300 000 tonnes a year of seamless steel pipe – despite the fact that its output will almost certainly be more expensive than comparable imports, has been justified on the grounds that it is geared exclusively to supplying the local oil and gas production industry (a captive market), which should ensure that it will be able to cover its financial costs while saving foreign exchange. (It would also probably pass muster under the GATT – thanks to the 'infant industry' or development clauses of Article XVIII.) Yet the problem with both these projects is that in a world where the markets for the products concerned are already, in global terms, more than saturated, the only effect of expanding productive capacity will be to depress prices and threaten the viability of existing suppliers, many of whom have themselves only recently undertaken similar investments.

One national steel industry which has been, most conspicuously, both a contributor to and a victim of this ill-considered expansion is that of Brazil. Following the government decision at the beginning of the 1970s to make steel a central component of its plans for industrial growth, by the end of the decade the productive capacity of the industry had been raised nearly threefold – to 18 million tonnes. This had originally been expected to result in only about a 10 per cent surplus for export. However, with domestic economic growth faltering, home demand fell to 12.3 million tonnes in 1980 – from a peak of 14.5 million tonnes – and has since fallen to as little as 10 million tonnes while capacity and output have continued to grow. More serious yet is the amount of surplus capacity still under construction but for which no markets either exist or are in the remotest prospect. In one instance this has produced a situation where the Brazilian government has felt obliged – rather in the manner of East European countries – to try and induce the equipment suppliers and their bankers (mainly British and West German) to accept the future products of the uncompleted project in part payment for the plant itself, for which financial resources are otherwise exhausted. This in turn has compelled the contractors – who are faced with the alternative of project cancellation and the loss of billions of dollars worth of business – to seek outlets for the products (mainly steel billets) in other countries. Although they have in fact succeeded in securing such advance agreements – as a security for new loans to facilitate completion of the project – it is clear that this has only been done on terms which imply a heavy discount on already depressed world prices. Thus instead of taking the otherwise logical decision to abandon the project another 1 million tonnes or more of product is to be added to the world surplus, thus still further postponing the day when something approaching stability can be expected to return to the world market.

Vicious circle in Brazil

No steel producing country can be more conscious of the vicious circle in which the industry is trapped than Brazil itself. For its own heavy investment in the sector in a very short period contributed significantly to the subsequent and continuing high level of the economy's overall indebtedness to foreign creditors. In order to service this debt, or merely to prevent it from growing any bigger, the country has to devote an increasingly high proportion of its now stagnant national product to exports (while also cutting back heavily on imports) so as to obtain the necessary foreign exchange. In consequence the country has been compelled to utilize its vast surplus of steel capacity to maximize export sales even at prices which are clearly unremunerative, since they still make a net contribution to the balance of payments (the foreign debt on the investment has of course to be serviced in any case). Yet they have also resulted in massive losses for the largely state-owned industry, so that by early 1984 the state holding company Siderbras was reportedly in debt to the equivalent of $7 billion. By thus in effect subsidizing its exports on to a world market which is already oversupplied it has inevitably acted to depress prices further, thus encouraging other countries with a similar desperate need for foreign exchange to act in a similar fashion. Failing an upturn in the world economy,[2] this process can only serve to aggravate the global market imbalance and operating losses up to the point where some governments (whether those of LDCs which are funding the losses of their steel producers directly or those of developed countries which are channelling subsidies through banks or suppliers of equipment) find they can no longer sustain the financial burden of the subsidies involved and the companies which depend on them are forced to the wall – with unpredictable economic and social consequences.

CRISIS IN THE OECD INDUSTRY

Steel industries in the developed countries have not, of course, escaped the effects of this squeeze. As noted above, there was heavy investment in new and expanded capacity in Western Europe and Japan in the first half of the 1970s, though less so in the United States. To some extent these outlays strengthened the ability of the producers concerned to resist the impact of recession, since the more modern plant could in many cases be operated profitably at lower levels of capacity utilization. However, this advantage was more than offset by the fact that their overall capacity was at the same time greatly increased against a background of falling demand. Indeed steel is a classic example of the tendency – which is common to a great deal of modern manufacturing – for modernization to entail expansion of capacity.[3] The result has been a steady accumulation of losses, particularly in Western Europe, where as a result governments have more and more been forced to intervene by way of either subsidizing or effectively nationalizing much of the industry (in Britain and Italy the state was already the dominant force in the industry before 1973). Despite extensive plant closures, notably in Britain and France, the combined net losses of the main steel producers of these two countries together with those of Italy, Spain and West Germany were running at an annual rate of some $5 billion in 1983, with little prospect of making any sizeable reduction in them without far more drastic cuts in capacity than any yet envisaged.

The response – subsidy, rationalization and price fixing
The Community has in fact been attempting to organize a collective response to this crisis of mounting overcapacity and operating losses ever since the problem was first clearly identified in 1976. Its approach has been based primarily on encouraging cuts in productive capacity spread among all member countries, coupled (since 1980) with a supposedly temporary system of output quotas – that is, effectively trying to cartelize the market. The trouble is that European demand has meanwhile fallen even further, and the scope for offsetting this by increasing exports is limited by a combination of the expansion of low-cost capacity in the LDCs and intensifying protectionist pressures in the United States, the biggest single export market of all. The LDCs – and in particular NICs such as South Korea and Taiwan – have in fact aggravated the problem further by making significant inroads into the EEC market, despite the low level of EEC prices made possible by heavy state subsidies. The fact that the Community has hitherto chosen to try and resolve its difficulties mainly by means of subsidy and internal control of the market rather than by taking an overtly hostile line against imports from third countries is doubtless to be explained by the fact that the EEC is still a substantial net exporter and wishes to minimize the risk of provoking retaliatory action.

The net result of these efforts was that by the end of 1982 the Council of Ministers was forced to accept that there was still a need to reduce the Community's steel-making capacity by over 30 million tonnes – or around 20 per cent. The practical lack of enthusiasm for implementing this target, however, led in late 1983 to the introduction of another stop-gap measure – in the shape of a regime of minimum prices – designed to cut the continuing financial losses and give the industry more breathing space with a view to ending all subsidies by the end of 1985 – a target which none the less seems hopelessly unrealistic.

US cartelization becomes the pattern

In fact it is striking that the pattern of steel protectionism in the EEC is coming gradually to resemble that of the United States, where cartelization and price fixing have long been entrenched. Such an approach – with the emphasis on preventing prices from falling rather than subsidizing production costs – is an inevitable choice for any US industry threatened by foreign imports, given the traditional American repugnance for directly subsidizing the costs of the private sector or, still more, for anything which could be construed as nationalization. This desire not to appear to be in open breach of the free market principles of which US business and political leaders are always such voluble champions no doubt also explains why, despite its relatively long history,[4] the system of protection is still operated in a largely informal fashion on the basis of a series of bilateral gentlemen's agreements. Such agreements are usually reached after a prolonged bout of arm-twisting in which the foreign supplier is subjected to threats of anti-dumping lawsuits and other measures designed to cut, or even eliminate, its exports to the US. This generally leads to a deal whereby the offending country quietly agrees to exercise 'restraint' – either by limiting the volume of its exports to the US or else undertaking not to sell any of the product concerned at prices below an agreed level – in return for the dropping of any action against it.

The net result of this process is to prevent importers, both individually and collectively, from taking too large a share of the US market, while ensuring that they have more or less guaranteed (if limited) access to the market at prices which are higher than those they would have received under a free-for-all. It is thus better designed to buy off dangerously competitive overseas suppliers, who would be only too well equipped to engage in a destructive price war. Indeed, in so far as it emphasizes the need to try and stabilize prices at something approaching viable levels for producers, it is theoretically a far more rational and effective form of protection than EEC-style subsidization, which merely tends to precipitate ruinous and unpredictable bouts of price undercutting (although its practitioners obviously cannot themselves defend it in these terms, since they are ideologically committed to pretending that they are not engaging in any form of protectionism, or that if they are it is only in retaliation for the market-distorting practices of others).

If it were not itself able to obtain such relatively high prices – which have in recent years often been as much as 30 per cent more than those prevailing in the rest of the world, it is obvious that the US steel industry would have been in even more serious trouble than it has, since its production costs are certainly now among the highest in the world, owing to a combination of relatively old and inefficient plant and high wage costs. The combined effect of lack of competitiveness and recession had the effect of halving US output between its peak in 1973 and 1982, when its production of only 67 million tonnes was actually lower than that of Japan – though it has since recovered slightly under the influence of the general revival of the US economy from the beginning of 1983. In fact the bulk of this fall in US steel output is undoubtedly attributable to the recession rather than to keenly priced imports. For what is most striking, in view of its own high prices and of the explosion of steel production among dollar-hungry LDCs – not to mention Europe's intractable surplus of capacity – is that the US industry has managed to withstand the onslaught from importers without surrendering a much larger share of its home market to them. Thus the fact that the share of imports in the US steel market rose only from 13 to 17 per cent between 1973 and 1983 despite the domestic industry's lack of competitiveness is a telling comment on the effectiveness of the protectionist methods described earlier.

Even so, while it is true that this approach has enabled the major US steel firms to avoid losses on the massive scale suffered by their European counterparts, it has not prevented them from registering mounting deficits and has certainly not guaranteed their long-term survival in other than a very truncated form. Consequently, just as the EEC is showing signs of moving towards US protectionist practice by placing more emphasis on quotas and price mainte-nance, the US industry has been belatedly forced to take a leaf out of the European book and draw up plans for a major rationaliza-tion of production – through a combination of plant closures and modernization. Furthermore the logic of cutting the industry down to a more viable size clearly also implies the need for corporate mergers – something which is already beginning to occur, though only with the benefit of some discreet relaxation of the anti-trust regulations, as in the case of the controversial plan (announced in

1983) for a merger of Republic Steel (the fourth largest US producer) and the steel-making plants of LTV. (This deal was originally blocked by the Justice Department on anti-trust grounds, but was subsequently permitted to go through following an outcry in the industry and an agreement on a few minor divestments of assets by the merging groups.)

Joining forces with Japan

More significantly, US steel companies have also begun to seek collaboration with Japanese producers, something which – as the motor industry has also discovered – is much less likely to be seen as anti-competitive than a takeover of or by another American organization (while, as already noted, neither the GATT nor any other set of United Nations rules makes any provision for coming to grips with the development of monopolies or oligopolies on an international basis). For a long time such collaboration was largely confined to technical cooperation agreements between Kawasaki Steel – one of the big four Japanese steel makers – and, respectively, Bethlehem Steel and Republic Steel. In 1984, however, it was announced that Nippon Kokan (NKK) – the world's third largest steel producing company and second in Japan – was to acquire a 50 per cent holding in National Steel, the fifth largest US producer and twentieth in the world – after the Justice Department had defeated an earlier move by US Steel to take over National completely.

For the financially beleaguered US industry there is perhaps no longer much alternative to such cooperation, which has the advantage of bringing them know-how as well as much-needed equity capital. For NKK, and perhaps in future for other Japanese steel groups, the attraction is obviously the opportunity to circumvent the limitation on its imports into the US – which have actually resulted in a decline of about 50 per cent in Japanese steel exports to the US since 1976 – and particularly to exploit the boost to US demand which it is anticipated will result from the establishment of large-scale production of Japanese cars in the United States.

NO ALTERNATIVE TO COLLABORATION

No one could possibly suggest that the hand-to-mouth protectionist measures described have yet come near to stabilizing the markets affected, let alone the world market as a whole. One conclusion, however, emerges quite clearly. This is that, despite all the brave talk of the need for free and fair competition, no major steel producer in the world is really prepared to accept the consequences of past follies and submit to the dictates of market forces. Instead both company chairmen and government leaders are coming to appreciate that collaboration and a sharing of burdens constitute the only possible response to the crisis which will not be unacceptably destructive. Nevertheless, as the continuing market imbalance testifies, it remains open to doubt whether those with the power of decision in all the countries involved will prove able to act with sufficient speed, honesty and cohesion to avert the still looming threat created by the anarchic development of the recent past.

NOTES

(1) UNIDO/International Centre for Industrial Studies, *Summary of the Draft World-wide Study of the Iron and Steel Industry: 1975-2000*. Vienna. November 1976.

(2) Even this might only be of limited benefit to the steel industry, as many industries – such as motor vehicles and canned beverages – have in recent years begun to replace steel with other materials, such as plastics, ceramics and aluminium, for certain applications.

(3) B. Keeling, *The World Steel Industry – Structure and Prospects in the 1980s*. London. *The Economist* Intelligence Unit 1983.

(4) Japanese steel exports to the US have been subject to effective restraint since 1968.

CHAPTER 9

The Inevitability of Managed Trade

It is to be hoped that the reader will by now have been convinced not merely of the utter irrelevance of the swelling chorus of demands for a 'return' to free or open trade but also of the danger of continuing to conduct the debate about international economic relations in terms of a theoretical choice between free trade and protectionism which in reality does not exist. However, if we are to proceed from these essentially negative conclusions to the formulation of the basis for a more useful and politically acceptable structure of world trade, it is appropriate to recapitulate the most salient findings of the preceding chapters.

One of the recurring themes of our analysis has been the total lack of any solid evidence for the existence of international free trade, other than in a very archaic and limited sense, throughout the period since World War II – or indeed in any period since the Industrial Revolution. The illusion of free trade in the post-war era has only been created by, firstly, equating it with the sharp reduction, now approaching total elimination in many OECD countries, of formal tariffs or quotas on imports, and then by the adoption of measures which made it possible for countries to accept the lowering of these traditional trade barriers without unduly exposing themselves to the unpredictable fluctuations of world market forces. The reality of the industrialized world since 1945 has been that countries have been far more committed than at any previous time to the belief that the unhindered operation of market forces could not assure adequate or sustained collective prosperity, and that the use of state intervention to control and manipulate these forces was not only the right but the duty of a responsible national government.

The paradox of seeking, in such a climate of world opinion, to establish a universal structure of free trade on a far more comprehensive basis than had ever previously existed is probably attributable in the first instance to the dissenting attitude of the United States – which happened to be the arbiter of the West's economic destiny in the aftermath of World War II. For the USA, despite its own strongly protectionist history and its experience of interventionism – by no means obviously damaging – under Roosevelt's New Deal and during the war itself, was ideologically averse to the idea of institutionalizing interference with the free market. Moreover, and perhaps most crucially, it recognized – like Great Britain a century before – that it was for the first time in a position of overwhelming economic supremacy *vis-à-vis* the rest of the world and thus had an unrivalled opportunity to gain from trade liberalization.

The fact that the superficial liberalization which occurred under the GATT system also coincided – at least up to the early 1970s – with an unprecedented growth in trade and general prosperity throughout the industrialized market economies has induced a facile tendency to conclude that the latter was the consequence of the former, thus confirming what was supposed to be the classical doctrine of the beneficence of free trade. However, as a few more circumspect economists have recognized, it is difficult to demonstrate that the liberalization process has contributed much to the rapid growth of trade.[1] It is in fact just as plausible to claim that the stimulus to economic activity provided by interventionist policies based on the teachings of Keynes lent the main impetus to the expansion of trade by creating a degree of confidence among both entrepreneurs and consumers which had been lacking in earlier phases of the capitalist epoch.

On this judgment the significance of the GATT is reduced to that of having diminished existing obstacles to trade so as to accommodate the desire to expand it, on the understanding that there were always means available to staunch the flow of imports should it prove embarrassingly large in relation to exports – or even, at the microeconomic level, sufficiently damaging to one particular sector of a national economy to threaten its survival. In addition it is clear that a significant, though unquantifiable, proportion of the increase in international trade was the result of exchanges between subsidiaries of multinationals in different countries – transactions which could not in any sense be said to constitute free or open exchange, although they were undoubtedly facilitated by tariff reductions under the GATT.

However, in rejecting the notion that free trade is a precondition of prosperity – or even that, in the words of a recent British Trade Secretary, free trade has ever existed 'outside a textbook'[2] – it is important to avoid falling into the opposite conventional trap of assuming that the road of protectionism can lead to long-term salvation. For whatever reservations one may have as to the orthodox arguments in favour of 'free' trade, the economic history of the post-war world surely does confirm the view that the opportunity of engaging in trade with other countries makes possible the attainment of far higher levels of prosperity than would be the case under conditions of traditional protectionism or economic isolationism. What is at issue, therefore, is or should be not the advantages or otherwise of engaging in trade, but the mechanisms by which international exchanges are carried on.

DANGERS OF RANDOM INTERVENTION

As this book has attempted to show, many of the devices used to regulate or influence trade flows during the period in which the GATT system has been in operation have been both *ad hoc* in character and clandestine in execution – in the sense that they have purported to have objectives other than that of controlling trade (for example, the raising of tax revenue or the safeguarding of public health). The reason for this subterfuge – and for the lack of warning as to other more blatant evasions of commitments to open trading – is obviously the fear of exposure at being in breach of the GATT and of the possible consequences in terms of retaliatory action. The main problem with this devious approach is that its effects are inevitably unpredictable and thus damaging to the climate of confidence which is essential to the security of investments and the general stability of economic activity.

In the previous two chapters we have seen how, faced with a breakdown in this stability resulting mainly from a disruption in the previous steady growth of demand and from the associated monetary disorder, both governments and multinational companies have sought to restore limited stability through progressively greater interference with market forces in such a way as to subject a growing number of markets to cartelization and managed trade. Their success in achieving balanced or 'orderly' markets has to date been very limited for the most part, largely because their efforts to do so have been generally uncoordinated and conducted on a bilateral basis. Moreover, because they remain at variance with the spirit if not the letter of the GATT, there is a continuing propensity to act secretly in the negotiation and implementation of these arrangements, so that third parties are frequently unaware of their existence and are thus in danger of basing their own investment or expansion plans on assumptions as to export potential which may soon prove to be quite unrealistic. In this way the 'new protectionism' actually tends to exacerbate rather than cure market imbalances and thereby to perpetuate uncertainty and recession at the global level, even though it may have served to stave off immediate disaster for individual national industries.

It should be obvious that such an anarchic, hand-to-mouth approach to determining the pattern of world production and trade cannot endure indefinitely. For its continuation would mean that all criteria for investment decisions – such as a realistic appraisal of demand, costs and prices – will be rendered meaningless, as to a considerable extent they already have been. In their place we shall see predominating more and more such considerations as the need to avert the bankruptcy of a multinational company or bank, to prevent massive job losses in a politically sensitive locality or to sustain in power the government of a strategically important developing country. The eventual outcome of such economic *anomie* remains unpredictable. Yet the increasing misallocation of resources which results from it can surely only be expected to aggravate wider economic problems and the associated political tensions, particularly as OECD taxpayers are called on to pay a higher and higher price – while non-taxpayers endure a gradual erosion of social services – for trying to sustain the ultimately unsustainable. It should therefore be of small comfort to critics of the market system to see a general flight from *laissez-faire* principles when they recognize that there is in fact no valid alternative in sight and every danger that this crisis of the international market economy will degenerate into the kind of disorder which characterized the 1930s – or worse.

THE FANTASY OF LIBERALIZATION

Yet equally, in calling for an end to such manipulations and a return to more open markets, those groups who may be collectively described – for want of a better term – as the free trade lobby have evidently failed either to grasp the reasons why governments resort to such practices or in any event to recognize the likely consequences of their renouncing them and exposing themselves to the full blast of market forces. It is true that, as has been demonstrated all too clearly in the previous two chapters, the uncoordinated efforts of different governments and multinationals to shore up their respective industrial bases or balance sheets by means of subsidies or other restrictive practices – in the hope that either there will be an early upturn in the level of demand or else that their weaker competitors will be forced to drop out of the struggle – have to date only tended to exacerbate the problems of oversupply. However, simply to wipe the slate clean and submit fatalistically to the guidance of the 'hidden hand' of the market is manifestly impracticable for two main reasons.

In the first place, no country can afford to allow the existing source of its national wealth or the livelihood of its citizens to be whittled away by competition without a solid guarantee of something to put in its place. This is a point too often ignored by those protagonists of the Third World cause[3] who advance the proposition that by opening their doors to cheap imports from LDCs and thereby occasioning the rundown of much of their traditional industry the developed countries will stimulate growth in demand among the LDCs for the more sophisticated products and services which only the West (with its more advanced technology) can supply. Such an argument is altogether too theoretical and lacking in tangible certainty to be acceptable as a basis for policy. For even if a government could be convinced that in casting its bread on the waters in this fashion it would stand a reasonable chance of receiving the long-term benefits of high employment and living standards which neo-classical orthodoxy suggest should be its reward, it would still need to resolve the problem of how living standards were to be maintained during the transitional period – even assuming it could estimate with reasonable accuracy how great the cost of such adjustment assistance would be.

Secondly, the linkage between economic and military capability has become so clear and indissoluble in this age of high technology that it is inconceivable that any country seriously committed to securing its military independence will refrain from engaging in what it chooses to see as a strategic sector of industry out of consideration for such a frivolous factor as international comparative costs of production. Indeed the right of countries to exclude trade in military hardware from their commitment to open and non-discriminatory trade is specifically recognized in the GATT (Article XXI) – a concession which, by extension, can reasonably be assumed to extend to the right to subsidize any industry designed to strengthen national security (in the narrowest sense of the term). Yet precisely because military strength and independence have come to depend on the ability to develop and apply the most advanced forms of industrial technology it is now no longer possible, if it ever was, to regard military-related production as of marginal significance in relation to the bulk of economic activity – as the GATT seems to imply. Furthermore, as suggested earlier, the concept of national security (the term used in the GATT) has effectively been extended – if not in conscious exploitation of the GATT loophole – to cover strategic considerations in the broadest sense, with the result that governments tend increasingly to define almost anything (such as, for example, the need for an independent source of supply of vital materials or components) as a vital national interest and therefore warranting protection or subsidization in some form or another. It can thus confidently be predicted that few if any governments will be persuaded to limit subsidies to projects with a definable military connection, given the undue advantage this could confer on those with the highest levels of direct military expenditure (anyone advocating an attempt thus to narrow the scope for subsidization on strategic grounds would, moreover, have to defend themselves against the charge of stimulating expenditure on armaments – that is, to provide a genuine excuse for subsidies thought desirable for broader economic or commercial reasons.) It is still less plausible to imagine that the United States would agree to cut back on its military-related R & D expenditure, or that its allies would really want it to, in the face of the continuing preceived threat from the

Soviet Union – which itself of course would find the whole concept of subsidy totally meaningless in terms of its own economic system.

Finally, and most decisively, the pattern of world production and trade which has developed under the cumulative impact of the various distortions of market forces that have occurred over the years is such as to preclude any systematic collective move to get rid of them. This is because these subsidies effectively guarantee the existence of a whole number of investments and enterprises which would cease to be viable in the absence of such protection and whose consequent demise would have incalculable economic and financial consequences – the impact of which would be all the more devastating in a climate where mass unemployment is already a desperately serious and apparently intractable problem (see later in this chapter). In short, to propose eliminating these distortions is to advocate a mass destruction of productive capacity, of financial assets and of livelihoods which, without the prospect of some means of immediate economic reconstruction on a more rational basis, would indeed be too awful to contemplate.

THE MICAWBERIST ALTERNATIVE

This last point is undoubtedly recognized by all but a tiny minority of *laissez-faire* fanatics. In other words, even mainstream right-wing politicians – including, for example, the Thatcher administration in Britain – accept that, however deplorable they may find the interventionist policies which they see as having brought the world economy to its present pass, they have no choice in the short run but to live with the status quo. In the longer term the best hope of this school of political thought appears to be that a recurrence of growth in the world economy will somehow be brought about – whether as a result of their supposedly monetarist policies or by some mystical process of spontaneous transformation – and that this will permit countries to relax their protectionist stance and progressively dismantle the interventionist superstructure. To be fair, however, it should be said that their political opponents on the left have equally tended to fall back on wishful thinking (reminiscent of Mr. Micawber's irrepressible confidence that 'something will turn up'), though in their case the longed-for revival of growth is supposed to be made more likely by still more intervention –

consisting mainly of a general increase in public spending designed to stimulate stagnant demand. They persist in this belief despite all the evidence since the early 1970s as to the limitations of this approach and its serious inflationary dangers (average rates of inflation in the OECD area in 1984 are still no lower than their 1971 level despite the trebling in the rate of unemployment).

Pending the advent of this long-promised saviour (that is, a return to growth) it has become increasingly common to hear calls for at least a freeze or moratorium on new measures of subsidization, cartelization or other instruments of the 'new protectionism'. Such a truce was first proposed by the Australian Prime Minister, Mr Malcolm Fraser at the GATT ministerial meeting of November 1982. It is no reflection on him that the idea fell largely on deaf ears, though one might have supposed that a realistic appraisal of the causes of and political attitudes to the new protectionism would have suggested that there was never any prospect of such a freeze being agreed to by even a significant minority of countries. For it should be clear that the purpose of the various market-distorting measures which aroused Mr Fraser's concern is precisely to compensate for the disadvantages which individual countries feel they suffer from, either as a result of other countries already having taken similar measures or because they feel themselves to be inherently and seriously handicapped in a way which the GATT rules fail to allow for. This being the case, it would seem *a priori* implausible that those countries which have hitherto abstained (or claim to have) from resorting to such protectionist measures to the same degree as others – whether overall or in relation to particular industries – would be willing to freeze the position at the status quo. For they may well believe, quite reasonably, that the disadvantage in which such a self-denying ordinance might place them would lead to the destruction of some of their key industries or the loss of export markets which are a vital source of foreign exchange.

THE UNEMPLOYMENT CONUNDRUM

The attitude of national governments to any suggestion that they should make sacrifices of this kind in the interests of international order and prosperity – very sensitive at the best of times – naturally tends to be all the more negative in a period when the level of domestic unemployment is as high as it has become in virtually all OECD countries in the 1980s. Indeed it is obvious that, for OECD countries in particular, rising unemployment has been the principal factor behind increased political pressure for protectionism. Recognition of this fact brings us back full circle to the view that the only way out of the protectionist impasse is via a return to sustained high rates of economic growth – that is, comparable to those experienced in the 1950s and 60s.

The question of whether or how such a restoration of growth might be effected – if indeed it is something which can be determined by policy actions of any kind – is one into which it would be inappropriate to enter here, although one is entitled to be extremely sceptical, as we have just suggested, as to the chances of this being achieved by any of the remedies currently on offer. However, even if one concedes the possibility that there may be a sustained revival of growth on a more or less global basis, there is powerful evidence to suggest that this will not solve the problem of unemployment and will thus not make the abandonment of protectionism – in the sense of a return to at least the relative openness of trade practised in the 1960s – any more acceptable or likely.

The reason for such pessimism is primarily the growing evidence that technological unemployment, so far from being the myth which many previously imagined it to be, has now become the principal source of the remorseless rise in joblessness. That is to say that in a large number of industries, in both manufacturing and service sectors, the progressive introduction of the new technology has sharply reduced the requirement for labour per unit of output and shows every sign of continuing to do so. Against such a background of soaring productivity, accompanied by a continuing growth in the size of the labour force (if at a slower rate than in the 1960s and 1970s – at least in the OECD) there can be little doubt that real economic growth would need to be sustained at much higher levels than ever achieved in the past – perhaps as much as 6 per cent a year, compared with under 4.5 per cent for the whole of the 1950-73 period – if unemployment is not to remain a major problem, such as to compel governments to adhere to a fairly protectionist stance in their policies on trade and industry.

The improbability of such high sustained growth rates being

attained in the OECD area is reinforced by the fact that the LDCs in general (and the NICs in particular) will continue their efforts to obtain a bigger share of world markets – for services such as shipping[4] and insurance as well as manufactures. While this will continue to benefit OECD suppliers of capital equipment of the more sophisticated type it will inevitably continue to have the opposite effect on manufacturers of consumer products and of intermediate goods such as steel and petrochemicals. In this way the Third World question should force the West to see its unemployment problem in a wider perspective. For just as employment has been the key to adequate living standards (or at least to a relatively satisfactory distribution of income) in the industrialized countries, so the lack of it – on anything like a regular basis – for most citizens of LDCs has been one of the classic symptoms of their economic backwardness and mass impoverishment.

But if the global problem cannot be solved by the traditional panacea of growth it is just as clear that the other most widely canvassed solution – that of cutting real wages – will be no more efficacious in cutting unemployment, even though it might theoretically be more feasible to implement – if political opposition to it can be overcome. As suggested in chapter 7, even many committed adherents of *laissez-faire* shrink from the idea of applying the ultimate logic of their free market ideas to wages, with all this would entail in terms of social distress and possible unrest (not to mention its depressive impact on the level of aggregate effective demand). Moreover, many probably also recognize that the notion of a market-clearing level of wages – i.e. one low enough to induce employers to take on all the available labour – is no more than an academic construct, devoid of any practical relevance in the real world, particularly in the industrialized countries. Above all it wholly ignores the fact that companies which have undertaken heavy investment in plant and machinery based on high capital and low labour intensity are most unlikely to write it off and revert to labour-intensive production methods even if the price of labour dropped to a fraction of its current level. The reason for this is not only that to do so would in most cases entail substantial capital losses but that there would be no guarantee that the relative cost of labour would not rise again, whereas the cost of using machines, once installed, is far more predictable – as indeed is their performance.

Furthermore, it should be clear that any entrepreneur who puts his faith in labour-intensive or 'intermediate technology' production methods as a viable basis for long-term competitiveness seems bound to conclude that, other things being equal, he would have a more durable prospect of profitable operation of this type in the LDCs, where both organized labour and legally imposed minimum standards for wages and other conditions of employment are less likely to be inhibiting factors.

It is therefore apparent that, faced with the virtual certainty of insufficient growth to absorb a labour supply rendered ever more abundant by accelerating productivity growth, and with the impracticability of bringing the demand for and supply of labour into balance through the price mechanism, the only way of combating mass unemployment will be through the effective rationing of work – probably accompanied by a radical advance in the use of the welfare state as a vehicle for income distribution. Precisely how social security systems might be transformed to cope with the need to channel an increasing flow of transfer payments to the growing proportion of unemployed or underemployed in industrialized societies is thus a question which seems certain to come to the forefront of political debate in the closing years of the twentieth century. (Space precludes a detailed consideration of this issue. However, it may be noted in passing that one answer to the question of how the higher welfare payments will be funded is through the reduction of company profits to take account of the virtual elimination of risk in investment.)

It is perhaps too early to speculate on the likely pattern of change in this field. It seems probable, however, that the implicit obligation of individuals to spend at least part of their lives in gainful employment is likely to be retained as a condition of receiving the benefits of the welfare state. If this is so, mechanisms for work sharing will need to be developed over an increasingly wide spectrum of economic activities.[5]

Moves in this direction – in the form of demands for shorter working hours, longer holidays and earlier retirement – have already been in evidence in Western Europe since the mid-1970s (notably in Belgium, the Netherlands, Britain and West Germany). Seen in historical context this would seem to be a logical and not particularly revolutionary approach to the problem, since it merely amounts to accelerating a process which has in any case been under way more or less continuously since the Industrial Revolution, and particularly since World War II. Yet progress towards a basic 35-hour week – the common goal of trade unions within the EEC, where the current average is around 40 hours – is being hindered by strong opposition from employers and a noticeable lack of enthusiasm on the part of governments.

In fact, such resistance should surprise no one, given that so many companies have since the mid-1970s been faced with a severe squeeze on their profits and a chronically harsh competitive environment in their markets, both at home and internationally. It is this need to remain competitive which has made it difficult for employers to make significant concessions in relation to the demand for a shorter working week, forcing them to insist that any reduction which is not accompanied by a pro rata cut in pay will force up unit costs and compel them either to squeeze profits or lose market share. Equally many workers – whether trade unionists or not – are reluctant to accept a cut in their real incomes, which have likewise been held down in recent years. The point which has scarcely been addressed by either side is that this impasse results from a pattern of international competition which is wholly distorted and increasingly destructive.

The prevailing view in government and business circles in Western Europe – and *a fortiori* in the United States, where such ideas apparently seldom get aired at all – is that these competitive constraints effectively rule out the use of work sharing as a viable answer to unemployment. Yet the idea refuses to die, and indeed seems certain to be advanced more insistently as the prospect of a sustained revival of rapid growth loses credibility. In that event the compelling need to implement some form of work sharing in a way which will not compromise the viability of enterprises which are exposed to international market pressures may well prove to be the catalyst for a more general recognition of the need for controlled international trade.

This possibility can only be strengthened by the ever growing tendency for governments and companies to agree that cut-throat competition has become a futile and dangerous process whose consequences are no longer acceptable. For if it is thought reasonable, on these grounds, to cartelize markets for steel, chemicals and other manufactures in chronic oversupply – not to mention those for primary products, such as tin and sugar, which have long been subject to attempts at cartelization and control for the purpose of ensuring reasonable stability of supply and price for the benefit of producers and consumers alike – it may be difficult to resist claims that labour is a commodity that is also a suitable case for cartelization. On the other hand, the implications of attempting to impose any controls on the supply and price of labour internationally are clearly momentous, given that cheap labour is the basis of whatever competitive advantage most LDCs have in international trade. It would thus be unrealistic to try and impose conformity through the promulgation of some code of practice sponsored by the ILO or other United Nations agencies. Rather it would be necessary to approach the question in the context of a broader examination of the 'international division of labour', which recognized the need to determine the allocation of economic resources between countries on a more rational basis than that provided by the crude and superficial criteria of short-run comparative costs.

But if both experience and reason point to a growing recognition of the inevitability of controlled trade as part of a more systematic attempt to regulate the world economy in the interests of a greater proportion of its people, it would clearly be naïve to suppose that this dawning perception will be easily or quickly translated into the political will to make this a reality. Indeed it could be argued that the political and ideological balance of forces in the Western World is now less propitious than it has been for many years to any proposals for a greater degree of collaborative planning either nationally or internationally. Whether or not this is true – or in any event will remain so for much longer – there will certainly be powerful forces continuing to argue publicly that free international competition is both desirable and capable of being restored, even though the protagonists of this view are often numbered among those private sector interests which have received most lavish support from the taxpayer.

THE INADEQUACY OF ORTHODOX TRADE THEORY

Yet the inconsistencies of so many of the leading spokesmen of the *laissez-faire* cause – which result from the basic contradiction of trying to uphold the values of the free market while also seeking to avert the more negative consequences of applying them – also lead one to suspect that the holes in their ideological defences will ultimately be so numerous as to make it impossible to shore them up any longer. In that event they may, along with many of their supporters among academic economists, come to accept that there is in fact nothing in orthodox economic theory which demonstrates that international trade needs to be free to be beneficial.

Indeed the essence of trade theory, based on the doctrine of comparative advantage, is that it will pay a country to trade with other countries to the extent that it will make possible a more economical use of its own factors of production – and thereby achieve a higher national average level of living standards – than would be the case if its economy was to remain entirely self-contained. At a rudimentary level of world economic development, where there were few industrialized countries and the vast majority were engaged mainly in primary production, this theory is a logical enough explanation for international exchange – as to why, for example, Britain has traditionally imported lamb from New Zealand and rubber from Malaysia (and exported manufactured goods to them in its turn) instead of relying on its own resources to produce all its lamb or (artificial) rubber, a choice which would demonstrably have meant lower economic efficiency and living standards compared with the effects of importing them. In a more complex world – in which there are both more industrialized (or industrializing) countries and greater scope, thanks to technology, for substituting traditional raw materials and increasing the productivity of agriculture in European countries which have in the past been relatively inefficient in that sector – comparative advantage inevitably tends to be less obviously inherent and more artificial. Above all it depends on the ability to deploy large amounts of capital on research and development and other assets designed to give countries (or companies) a superior capability in key areas of advanced technology. Where, as is now almost invariably the case, state subsidies play a crucial role in creating these advantages it is inevitable that they will fail to be regarded as genuine or permanent by other countries – particularly where the latter feel that their own comparative advantage has been distorted by market manipulation of one kind or another.

Above all, however, the relevance of orthodox trade theory is limited by the chronic and massive excess of supply over demand for productive factors – particularly labour.[6] This, it must be emphasized, is not in any sense a recent phenomenon, although from the end of World War II up to the early 1970s it could be described as a latent one in the eyes of the Western industrialized nations. For the developing nations of the Third World, however, it was and remains a perpetual reality. What has now become clear – as indicated earlier – is that, even with sustained world-wide growth rates far higher than those attained in the 1950s and 1960s, it is inconceivable that it will be possible to absorb the global supply of manpower into the labour market on the basis of what is conventionally understood as full (that is, full-time) employment.

COLLECTIVISM IS HERE TO STAY

Despite spirited efforts to keep alive a more optimistic view of the prospects for growth – usually based either on variants of Kondratieff's semi-mystical 'long wave' theory[7] or on the absurd and archaic doctrine known as Say's Law[8] – it is apparent that the message is gradually sinking in. Indeed it is clear from the pattern of modern trade and protectionism as described in earlier chapters that most governments and multinational companies have at last come to recognize that there is no possibility of achieving full employment of productive factors on a world scale except, at best, in the intolerably long run. This helps to account for the growing trend, referred to earlier, towards collaboration rather than competition in the pattern of commercial relations which is emerging in the 1980s. This development doubtless also reflects an increasing recognition of the futility and wastefulness of artificial competition – that is to say, fuelled by subsidy and having little or no relation to market realities. In this sense it could actually be said to be more in keeping with the spirit of the theory of comparative advantage – in other words, the optimization of use of resources – than is the system of supposedly open trade which it is implicitly rejecting. For it amounts to conceding that, in an age of highly capital-intensive production and of economies of scale that grow faster than demand, duplication of effort by companies or countries seeking each to have its own independent capability in the new high technology industries cannot be equated with the pursuit of economic efficiency.

Finally, therefore, the chief cause for hope of a concerted move towards a more effectively and rationally planned structure of world trade lies in the manifest bankruptcy of the more traditional models. Moreover, given that state intervention and the 'planning system' are already established features of national economies, to transpose this approach on to the international plane should not require a huge ideological upheaval. Indeed in these circumstances any residual cries for the maintenance or restoration of free trade will be increasingly conspicuous in their insincerity – no more than 'the facade of a dogma with solid interests behind it'.[9] Others will recognize that in seeking to impose some kind of order on the way in which market forces are controlled and manipulated they will merely be imitating a practice pioneered by multinational companies and (within their own frontiers) national governments. Yet they must also understand that the reason the latter have failed is precisely that they are compelled by the political exigencies of nation states and the remorseless competitive pressures of capitalism to operate largely in isolation, and that for this reason nationally based intervention in the market produces 'international instability and disintegration'.[10]

NOTES

(1) Cf. G. Ohlin, Trade in a non-*laissez-faire* world, in P.A. Samuelson (ed.), *International Economic Relations*. London. Macmillan 1969.

(2) Mr John Biffen, quoted in *Financial Times*, 7 April 1982.

(3) Cf. Brandt Commission, *North–South: A Programme for Survivial*. London. Pan Books 1980.

(4) The United Nations code of conduct on conference line shipping, finally inaugurated in November 1983, assures LDCs of the right to carry at least 40 per cent of their seaborne trade in vessels of their own national shipping lines.

(5) Cf. A. Gorz, *Farewell to the Working Class – an essay in post-industrial socialism*. London. Pluto Press 1982.

(6) As Professor Joan Robinson has pointed out, classical free trade theory assumes not only full employment, but the absence of migration of either labour or capital across frontiers, perfect mobility and adaptability of productive factors will frontiers, fixed exchange rates and, of course, perfect competition (J. Robinson, *The New Mercantilism*. Inaugural lecture at Cambridge University. Cambridge University Press 1966).

(7) This purports to show, on the basis of purely statistical evidence, that there is a long-term world economic cycle of around 50 years – which would mean that some dramatic resurgence of growth is more or less inevitable at some point before the end of this century. Nothing could better illustrate the poverty of contemporary economics than the fact that so many academics (and others) allow themselves to take this proposition seriously.

(8) Attributed to Jean Baptiste Say – an otherwise justly forgotten contemporary of Malthus and Ricardo – this is the belief that supply creates its own demand.

(9) J. Robinson, op. cit.

(10) G. Myrdal, *Beyond the Welfare State*. London. George Duckworth 1960.

CHAPTER 10

The Possible Shape of the Future

It will be apparent from the preceding chapters that many of the essential features of an international regime of planned trade are already present in existing methods of trade regulation, even if these are only applied in an *ad hoc* and usually quite informal fashion to trade in individual commodities. However, because of the powerful vested interests engaged in sustaining the notion that the present system of international exchange corresponds to an approximation of free trade – from which there have merely been some slight, though regrettable derogations – it would be some-what naïve to imagine that these symptoms of a more regulated approach can be viewed as signs of a gradual but ineluctable evolution towards multilateral planned trade on a global basis.

Yet perhaps it is not too fanciful to suggest ways in which certain existing practices might be adapted to form the basis of an evolving integrated structure of planned world trade, which would in turn make possible a less anarchic pattern of economic development in general. Two forms of trade management in particular appear both bound to be increasingly prominent features of the efforts of different countries to come to terms with the current combination of stagnation and instability – which on present trends will continue to plague the international economy for the foreseeable future – and to form part of any new regime of global trade organization to be established in place of the GATT. These are cartelization and barter trading.

CARTELIZATION

The progressive moves towards a more or less formal allocation of shares (by country) of the main export markets for steel – the USA and the EEC – could well constitute the rudiments of a model for efforts to stabilize other world markets in chronic oversupply, as could (in a slightly different way) the Multi-Fibre Agreement, which is designed to ensure the orderly expansion of textile and clothing exports to OECD markets from LDCs only (see chapter 7). In fact it is clear that many other markets for manufactured goods are already cartelized to a considerable extent – and will increasingly be so – as a result of the growing trend towards joint ventures and collaboration in marketing between multinational companies.

Indeed there is little doubt that, for example, the chemical companies of the Western World would have suffered far more than they have – in terms of financial losses – from the chronic oversupply of petrochemicals which has developed since the early 1970s but for the oligopolistic structure of marketing in this sector, controlled as it is by the oil majors and the other giant chemical groups such as Dupont, Bayer and ICI. This *de facto* cartelization of the petrochemical market – which is made easier, if not inevitable, by the high level of investment required in both production and distribution (thus posing considerable obstacles to potential new entrants) – considerably predates the post-1973 recession. For other industries which are less inherently protected it has been necessary to improvise new collaborative arrangements to cope with the intensifying competitive pressures of recession. Thus the joint venture approach, as noted earlier, is increasingly conspicuous in those sectors where survival in world markets has come to depend on huge outlays on either research and development (such as telecommunications equipment) or large-capacity new plant capable of realizing economies of scale (for example, the motor industry).

It would seem fairly predictable that other industries exposed to such high investment costs and correspondingly large risks will in the near future succumb to these pressures in favour of collaboration, and that, so far from being restricted in doing so by anti-trust and competition regulations, they will receive active official encouragement and assistance in such initiatives. Perhaps the most obvious candidates for such concentration of forces are those where Japanese producers have established a clear competitive edge but are facing pressure for restrictions on their exports, while their competitors have no prospect of catching them up without undertaking substantial investments of doubtful profitability. Examples of industries falling in this category are machine tools, typewriters, photographic equipment and electrical consumer durables. Indeed such collaboration is already a reality in the latter sector, as witness joint ventures between (respectively) Sony, Hitachi, JVC and others with various European partners to assemble television sets and video recorders for the EEC market.

Yet the essence of this type of inter-company cartelization is that it is, almost by definition, aggressive in intent as well as often being implemented in a clandestine manner. That is to say that it usually entails an attempt by major suppliers of particular sectors to carve up a substantial share of the market between them at the expense of their other competitors. For this reason, and also doubtless because they do not wish to give undue publicity to their efforts to increase their monopolistic market power, they naturally tend to keep their detailed plans as secret as possible. Unfortunately, however, in doing so they negate what might otherwise be regarded as the main public benefit of cartelization, namely the reasonable guarantee of predictability as to market shares and prices which are the indispensable conditions of both corporate and economic stability.

The clear lesson is that if cartelization is not simply to perpetuate the instability which it is intended to neutralize it must be structured so as to benefit all, or at least a substantial majority of, market participants – producers and consumers alike. It will only be able to do this if it is implemented quite explicitly, with the agreement of as many interested parties as possible and with the full authority of law behind it. This means that governments will need both to be involved in negotiating the terms on which cartels are established and to be the ultimate authority sanctioning them.

BARTER TRADING

Another device which, as noted in Chapter 7, has suddenly emerged as a popular (not to say vital) means of getting round the constraints imposed by the recession is that of barter or counter-trading. Its rapid growth since the late 1970s has been largely an *ad hoc* response to the chronic weakness of so many LDCs' balance of payments – thus confirming, in a sense, the textbook view that barter is a practice which occurs in conditions of monetary disorder where currency is either totally absent or has lost its acceptability as a medium of exchange. However, there is strong evidence to suggest that, in the eyes of many LDCs, the principle of matching reciprocity in bilateral trade relations is both a sound basis for ensuring a satisfactory external balance and, perhaps above all, their most potent weapon in compelling industrialized countries to import from them on relatively equitable terms.

As in the case of cartelization, it can safely be predicted that the scale of recourse to countertrade will continue to increase as long as the recession continues and particularly if, as seems inevitable, the external imbalance and indebtedness of LDCs increases further. However, again as with cartelization, countertrade cannot offer any basis for a durable stabilization of international economic relations as long as it is organized on a purely piecemeal, bilateral basis. On the contrary, it is all too likely that it will lead to even more disruption of established trade flows to add to that already wrought by recession and the debt crisis. Furthermore, if individual countries (or even trading blocs such as the EEC) pursue an increasingly bilateral approach to trade relations – that is, if they aim at achieving a balance in their exchanges with each of their trading partners severally – it will obviously impose rigidities which will deny them the potential benefits which could be obtained under a multilateral trade system.

On the other hand, once it can be overtly conceded that free trade is not, never has been and never can be a practical basis for determining the pattern of international exchange, it is self-evident that any new post-GATT international arrangement for trade regulation will have to take cognizance of the fact that trade flows (together with movements on invisible or capital account) must be such as to ensure that participating countries' external accounts are more or less balanced over the medium to long term – without the necessity to achieve this through the brutal market mechanism of an adjustment in the exchange rate or by submitting to chronic austerity imposed by international market fluctuations beyond their control. For if any country were to accept a position in which its balance of payments would be in structural deficit, it would by the same token be acquiescing in its subordination, political as well as economic, to the will of external powers. An alternative (or complementary) approach to this problem might be to compensate the more economically deprived countries with a system of permanent transfer payments from the more productive ones. Such an arrangement, which would be in line with one of the more imaginative recommendations of the Brandt Commission, could be seen as elevating the principle of regional policy, as applied by national governments, to a global scale.

The determination of international trade flows on the basis of such administrative mechanisms as cartelization and planned matching reciprocity (whether bilateral or multilateral) rather than on the basis of price would naturally impose the requirement to determine the prices of traded goods in a similar administrative fashion. Here once again there are precedents to provide some guidance as to how this issue is most likely to be addressed, although even if there were not it is fairly obvious that, in the absence of a freely determined market price, the only logical basis for price fixing is the cost of production. The use of Japanese cost coefficients as a basis for the US steel import trigger price mechanism – referred to in chapter 8 – is perhaps a significant, if somewhat crude, indicator of how this problem might be approached in the event of more global and multilateral cartelization of markets. Ultimately it would be necessary to establish price yardsticks based on rather more objective criteria of cost and efficiency, including – most crucially – the setting of wage and productivity standards for labour and the appropriate rate of return on capital employed.

In this connection the experience of national price control authorities in many OECD countries, such as the now defunct Prices and Incomes Board and the Price Commission in Britain, would clearly be relevant. It will, of course, be argued that the inability to establish satisfactory and durable criteria for wage and price levels in a purely national context was what doomed these earlier institutions to failure and ultimate extinction, and that therefore – *a fortiori* – it would be all the more impossible to achieve this in an international context. Since, however, the objective would in the first instance be to set minimum prices to apply to imports – rather than to control prices *per se* – it should be possible to arrive at agreed minimum levels which would be adequately remunerative to domestic producers without necessarily prejudicing the discretion of importers to increase their profit margins (or wage rates) while keeping their prices at or above the official minimum or 'trigger price' threshold. In any event it should be clear that there could be no question of a rapid move to fix international price standards for particular manufactures – even within a range – in the immediate future. What is far more plausible is that minimum import price criteria, based on a reasoned build-up of production and distribution costs, will be established in separate national or regional (for example, the EEC) markets – along with effective quota ceilings for individual supplying countries.

The need for transparency

As already implied, an insistence upon 'open agreements openly arrived at' – a latter-day application of one of President Wilson's Fourteen Points – would be an essential element in the implementation of a system of multilateral trade management. Apart from the necessity to avoid the present anarchic consequences of secrecy, this rule would be justified by the fact that the severe curtailment of competition (and thus of risk) implicit in cartelization would mean that any appeal to the requirements of commercial confidentiality would not be admissible. Moreover, it would assist the spread of information about markets and cost and price criteria, thus helping to provide a more rational basis for investment decisions by existing or potential new producers and reducing the possibility of ill-advised speculative investment in increased capacity to serve non-existent markets. (This dissemination of cost and productivity criteria would also be a help to organized labour in establishimg something approaching internationally agreed standards for terms and conditions of employment – something which the promulgation of ILO standards, which are ratified and implemented by governments on a more or less voluntary basis, has never begun to achieve in the competitive world environment which has prevailed hitherto.)

A DIFFERENCE OF PRINCIPLE

In the last few pages we have sought to illustrate how a move towards more systematically planned or managed trade could be initiated based upon existing practices. Yet it should be clear that, while an element of continuity could and should be present in any 'new order' of international economic relations designed to meet the needs of a rapidly changing world, a fundamental change of emphasis is called for. The essence of this change must be a more explicit recognition that the principle of competition needs to be regarded as subordinate to the requirements of equity and stability.

For if there is one lesson above all others to be learnt from the experience with the GATT system it is that no supposedly global regime governing world trade – or indeed international economic relations generally – can be durable if even a significant minority of countries come to see its provisions as being at variance with their interests. This is because such minorities will always tend to seek ways of pursuing their national objectives in ways which are liable to disrupt the market in the world at large. At the same time the GATT experience also points to the futility of attempting to construct any set of rules which could be universally applicable (that is, on a non-discriminatory basis) to countries with vast differences in their level of development and consequently in their endowment in technology and other factors of production. This is a reality which could perhaps more easily be ignored at a time, such as the 1950s and 1960s, when there seemed to be virtually no limit to the scope for economic growth and when it was possible to sustain the illusion that 'development' would sooner or later ensure that the LDCs caught up with the living standards of the industrialized West. Now that such optimism has been utterly banished it is surely obvious that no new set of rules of the game will be acceptable which is based on the assumption that all participants start on equal terms and with an equal opportunity to exploit opportunities in the world market.

In attempting to gain formal acceptance of the type of planned trade structure briefly outlined in this chapter – as a logical development from the existing pattern of anarchic distortions of the free market – it would also be essential to stress that cartelization and planned reciprocity are necessary precisely because there are limits to economic growth (not, it should be emphasised, in absolute terms, but in relation to the speed at which the world's actual and potential productive capacity is expanding and will continue to expand for the foreseeable future). Yet if that is so those nations – or indeed social groups – which are manifestly in a position of relative deprivation under the status quo are unlikely to accept that the distribution of economic activity, which heavily influences the distribution of income, as between countries and communities should be more or less immobilised according to the present pattern. Even to hint at such an idea would provoke an explosion of Third World outrage at what would justifiably be depicted as another attempt to divide the spoils of the world economy between the OECD countries and a few fortunate benficiaries among the NICs – not to mention increasing disaffection among the economically depressed sections of industrialized societies.

It would thus be a quite inescapable consequence of seeking to establish a global regime of planned trade that it should be linked to the creation of machinery for the collective allocation as between countries of productive capacity in the main economic sectors entering into international trade. In short there would have to be an understanding of the need to make cartelization respond to the requirements of equity rather than simply, as at present, those of expediency. Failure to do this will almost certainly mean that the present informal approach to cartelization will degenerate into something like the pattern of international economic aggression which characterised the 1930s and contributed so signally to the tensions which led to World War II.

Official endorsement of the idea that 'social' considerations should be given primary importance in the organization of the international economy would naturally have repercussions for domestic economic management. This should have the benefit of elevating economic debate above the sterile confrontation between the empty rhetoric of those who persist in urging the need for greater national competitiveness and, on the other hand, the crude, often xenophobic, demands for protectionism voiced by those whose jobs or businesses are threatened by the ruinous struggle for commercial dominance. Only in such a new climate would it be possible to overcome the desperate but understandable determination – often manifested in civil unrest – of steel workers in Belgium or coal miners in Britain to hold on to manifestly unnecessary jobs at all costs, and instead to redirect it into a constructive search for a rational and equitable disposition of productive capacity and economic resources on both a national and an international basis.

It will be clear that such an approach would imply a large step towards a structure of international organization which would treat the world economy as for most purposes a single entity. To many such a proposition will appear as utopian as it is, admittedly, banal. To those who have been reduced to a state of greater open-mindedness by their bafflement at the seemingly insoluble riddle of the world economic crisis it may occur that a change of this kind is not perhaps as radical as they might once have thought, at least in ideological terms. For, as has been emphasised throughout this book, the post-war period has witnessed the more or less general acceptance both of the vital necessity for a cooperative approach to international relations and of the necessity for state intervention in the economy if the more negative consequences of applying market forces are not to become intolerable. Thus an attempt to combine these two principles is arguably no more than a logical extension of received wisdom.

On the other hand it would be foolish to make light of the likely obstacles to any attempt to create a more comprehensively collaborative structure of world trade along the lines sketched out above. The tendency of much of the international establishment to insist upon the essential primacy of market forces, in the teeth of all the evidence of their own policies and behaviour, has already been frequently commented upon. Yet even if this rhetoric is wearing increasingly thin, there clearly remain real difficulties in the way of mobilizing political will in favour of such an open acceptance of international interventionism – difficulties which the vested interests opposed to any change can be expected to play on for all they are worth.

The prospect that the task of implementing and administering such a system might be entrusted to another United Nations bureaucracy, remote from any political control or responsibility, would certainly not be a hopeful one in the eyes of many, given both the obvious weaknesses of some existing UN agencies and the tendency on the part of the media in many countries to denigrate even their more commendable efforts. It is scarcely possible here to address the general question of how to reconcile the continuing claims of national independence – only recently attained by so many countries – with the ever more pressing requirements for international collaboration. It would seem clear, however, that any institutional structure established for the purpose would need, if it was to acquire a genuinely supranational authority, to be subject to a recognisable form of democratic control – a requirement which could clearly pose problems bearing in mind the largely unrepresentative nature of so many of the member governments of the United Nations.

In view of these undoubted difficulties, the best hope of finding a way forward may be through an initiative involving a limited nucleus of states – both developed and developing – in mutual cartelization, trade reciprocity and cross-border planning. Given the traditions of its member states, it would seem that the EEC might well be an appropriate vehicle for such an experiment, although it would have to seek partnership with a far weightier group of LDCs than the weak and fragmented collection of states at present associated with it under the Lomé Convention. However, if the danger of provoking a general movement towards mutually hostile trading blocs was to be avoided, it would have to be stressed from the outset that such a grouping was to be non-exclusive and open to new adherents – indeed that it was seen as merely a stepping stone on the road to a more global structure.

Quite clearly any moves in such a direction would amount to a radical departure in economic cooperation and economic management, and as such could easily fall foul of existing vested interests – often masquerading as the guardians of national traditions and institutions. For this reason it would seem unrealistic to expect any substantive effort to bring about international collective action of this kind except under the duress of imminent or actual economic collapse in those countries which at present dominate the non-Communist world. Sadly, it appears to be the lesson of earlier initiatives in the present century to promote greater international collective security that thay can only occur in response to the actual devastation of world war. Unless the present generation can summon the imagination to disprove this apparent truism it seems all too possible that the next generation will not survive to apply the moral of the failure of its predecessors.

Index